A LITTLE GIRL IN A WOMAN'S SHADOW

A TRUE STORY

BY

RUTH M. SPURLIN

authorHOUSE

1663 Liberty Drive, Suite 200
Bloomington, Indiana 47403
(800) 839-8640
www.authorhouse.com

First published by AuthorHouse 11/15/04

ISBN: 1-4184-5149-5 (sc)
ISBN: 1-4184-5150-9 (dj)

Library of Congress Control Number: 2004094297

Printed in the United States of America
Bloomington, Indiana

This book is printed on acid-free paper.

Some names have been changed to protect the innocent

DEDICATION

To my mother, my four children, five sisters and four brothers
For all their love. Support and protection.

FOREWORD

This epical account of the life of an individual and family living in a so called civilized cultural society will arouse the most profound questions ever imaginable. An absolute absence of constitutional protection for the individual. If it hadn't been for the courage and determination of this person to record as a public reference in her own way, sociology would have no benchmark to record the performance of our social institutions.

The breakdown in social order described in this TRUE STORY can only be accredited to gross neglect by elected officials who are entrusted with upholding the constitution and other laws of a civilized society. The problems only went away when the cause of the problems went away not by any directed action by institutional mandates. This lack of intervention by social order not only aggravated the abuses but provided absolutely no temporary or permanent solutions.

This book should be made mandatory reading for any serious sociology student. Joyce Ennis.

INTRODUCTION
Brutality, Murder, Rape and Incest

I have had three professional editors make attempts to edit the true story you are about to read. Each found the text too difficult to polish, The author admits that she is not a scholar and was not blessed with the opportunity to develop her writing skills. There lies the significance of the book you have chosen. The author may very well be like the girl next door or down the street or from any other village, town or city in America. One of the girls out of every forth girl who has suffered from violence and sexual abuse. And we all know that many abuse cases are forever kept behind closed doors, not the case in the abuse of Ruth Spurlin.

Her story should not be read for its literary correctness but for its blunt honesty. It should be read for the truth about the social issues this women survived through to move beyond the effects of the abuse she endured and the lasting effects it had on herself and her children. We should not glory in the freedoms our For-fathers fought to give us without realizing that we have failed to protect the weakest links of our society. When we allow the following to occur, when those in authority fail to act properly, we must take some of the blame and resolve to work diligently to decrease all levels of abuse. We who are humans, who being elevated above the angles, allow some among us to treat our weakest links as worse than dogs are treated. It is time for a change.

Through research, I was to discover that there were enough people, especially those in authority, who knew of this woman's blight. Knew of the torture yet did little or nothing to protect her, her children, her siblings, and her unborn child from the torture they endured much too long. Can a town and her professionals ever live down the shame it has brought upon itself? That question I have not as yet been able to answer without being too critical.

Dwight Wallington, Editor-Publisher

Chapter One

Mother always said, "Ruthie, life is what you make it, and, if you don't like it, change it." Yet my sister Erva told me that Mother couldn't help us kids because she had been brought up under the old standard that women had to stick it out, for better or worse. She felt she had to stick by Daddy even while he was ruining our lives. How we all got raised is a miracle.

I was born in Marietta, Indiana, in 1937, number ten out of eleven children.

Marietta was a small town of about five hundred people at the time. It had two small grocery stores and a gas station and was about ten miles from the bigger town of Shelbyville. Few homes had phones.

Most people used the telephone exchange located in a private home.

The town was small but busy. There were always people about. Kids on bikes or skates played on the roads. Adults and young people could be seen walking along the roads, in the grocery stores, at the gas station.

Buses filled with soldiers from Camp Atterbury would pass through the town on the way to Shelbyville for the weekend. The soldiers would holler at all the pretty girls they saw.

The town was clean and fresh. It seemed like there was always a fresh breeze blowing, and we left our windows and doors open so that it could blow through our houses. It was a nice place to grow up for a country girl like me.

I was born bow-legged, and Mother had wanted to take me to Indianapolis for treatment. But Daddy had said, "Marie, we can't do that. She will cry herself to death." I was a real Mommy's and Daddy's baby, Mother always said.

1

Mother and Daddy started pushing my legs as close together as they could, three or four times a week. Mother said I remained bow-legged for years and couldn't catch a pig if I had to, but that they had never given up working on my legs. Whatever they did sure worked. You can hardly tell today that I was ever bow-legged.

I had six sisters and four brothers. One of the girls, Mildred, died when she was only three weeks old. I never knew her, but I put flowers on her grave when I go home. Several of my brothers and sisters were grown and had moved out of the house when I was growing up.

My sister Erva left Shelbyville in 1943 and doesn't know a lot of the family history I remember. Mother and Daddy didn't know much about her life either after she left home. She said her life as a little girl consisted of toting her brothers and sisters on her hip, washing diapers, cooking and cleaning, or helping Daddy in his truck patch--weeding, hoeing, picking, and sorting cucumbers or whatever else there was to do. My sister Norma worked in Daddy's pickle patch too, picking cucumbers or tomatoes or pulling weeds. Daddy told her she was the best pickle puller he had.

We were very poor because my father, Hurley Spurlin, was an alcoholic. He was a fence builder by trade, and a good one. Everyone in Marietta wanted my daddy to build their fence. When he worked, he made good money, but we saw very little of it at home.

He could work only in spring and summer because the winters in Indiana were long and cold, and he couldn't dig post holes. Come summer, if Daddy didn't have a fence to build, he would plant a big garden. He grew potatoes, cucumbers, and other vegetables, which he took into town and sold from the back of the Model A Ford that he had converted into a truck by cutting the back of it off. What a sight that Model A was.

He had a big patch where he used to grow cucumbers the size of his little finger. He had a lot of customers who ordered his small cucumbers from year to year to make pickles. He used to take them to Shelbyville and put them on a train to wherever they went.

He didn't have a horse, so he plowed the garden by hand. He made a platform and loaded it with rocks to weigh down the plow, strapped it to a shoulder harness and pulled it himself. The rows he made would be straight as they could be. As far as his garden work went, everything he did had to be perfect.

In the winter, Daddy would buy a hundred chickens. They would come in on the train in boxes. By the time he picked them up, twenty or thirty of them would be dead. At home he would put them in the living room behind the potbelly stove to keep them warm. They would stay there about a month. They were incredibly noisy, and I was always glad when

Daddy would put them outside in the chicken coop. He would put a couple of coal oil lanterns in with them to keep them warm and put tar paper over the coop.

Daddy was tall and handsome. When he was sober, he was a kind and gentle man who wouldn't say a bad word about anybody. He used to say that if you couldn't say anything good about somebody you shouldn't say anything. Trouble was that he wasn't sober very often. When he was drunk, he was a different person I didn't know and was afraid of.

When I was a little girl, my daddy would sit in an old big chair beside the wood stove, and I would get up on his lap and go to sleep. Mother said he would then carry me to bed.

He never did spank me as I recall, but he sure did spank my brother Lloyd and sister Louise. He would put their heads in between his legs and spank away on them. And Erva said we younger children didn't know what she, Thelma, Albert, Jimmy, and Gene went through. Daddy was really mean to the boys. One time Daddy hit Jimmy in the nose, and it bled for days. The boys were afraid to go off anywhere if Daddy was drinking because they were afraid of what he would do to Mother while they were gone. Daddy kicked Gene out, and he went to live with Erva before joining the Army. I'd had no idea before talking to Erva that Daddy had abused the older kids that way. He had been good to my sister Glenda and me, maybe because he was older and sick at the time. I loved him until the day he died, but I couldn't understand his ways.

My mother, Marie Spurlin, was five feet tall and, we kids used to say, five feet around. She weighed about 160 pounds. She had a temper like a buzz saw and was a strict disciplinarian. When she got mad, you could see sparks fly out of her black eyes, and we would say it was the Indian coming out. She was part Cherokee Indian but never knew how much. Both my Kerr grandparents had Cherokee blood. They came from Kentucky, and Grandpa Kerr was a train conductor. Grandma Kerr was a beautiful lady and was a Harrison before she married Grandpa. She was related to President Harrison. She named my mother Siotha after an Indian chief's wife, but Mother never did like her name and changed it to Marie. Once I told her I'd like to name a daughter after her real name, and she had a fit. "Don't you dare, Ruthie," she said. "I hate that name."

She had been born in Amity, Indiana, the fourth of six children. When Mother was about four, something happened between her parents. She never knew what happened exactly, but one day her father dropped her, her sister Daisy, and brother Jesse off at a corner, pointed to where her sister Gertie lived, and told them to go there.

Aunt Gertie had three children of her own and couldn't keep all three of them. She kept Daisy but put Mother and Jesse in an orphans' home. Mother had stayed in the home until she was about twelve and then went to live with a Dr. and Mrs. White.

Mother called her parents by their first names, and one day I asked her why. She said she had never known them by any other name. I asked if her mother had ever been with her when she had us kids, and she said, yes, when she had Gene. Then she said, "Ruthie, I don't want to talk about my parents anymore." That was all I ever learned about her past.

We lived in an L-shaped house owned by a man I'll call Bill. Bill lived in two rooms in the long part of the L. We had three rooms in the short end, one bedroom, a living room, a small kitchen, and a big wash room where we took our baths in the summer. There was also a woodshed.

The house was surrounded by farmland, and in the summer all we could see were cornfields. When the corn was picked and the stalks cut down, we could see for miles. We had to pump water from a well and had a two-seat outside toilet that my daddy had built. We had an ice box, coal oil lamps, and a coal oil cooking stove. A potbelly wood stove provided the heat.

I remember hearing Mother tell Lloyd and Albert to stay in bed until Daddy got up and made a fire so Glenda and I could get ready for school. We would take a bath out of a wash pan in the winter behind the old potbelly stove.

I don't remember ever seeing my brothers or father naked. My mother made sure of that. There was one time when one of the mattresses caught fire in the bedroom. Albert slept naked I guess. He ran outside dressed only in his hat. We didn't see much. Mother had him back inside in a hurry.

There were three beds in the bedroom: Mother and Daddy's big old iron bed and a big bed for Albert and Lloyd. Glenda and I had a half bed against one wall facing the door to the living room. Glenda slept at one end, and I slept at the other. I think there was a cotton blanket covering the mattress but no sheets or top blankets. There was a row of coats that someone had given us hanging from nails on one wall, and every night Glenda and I would get three or four coats and put them on the bed to keep us warm, using one for a pillow. Every morning we had to hang them back up.

The plaster and wooden lathe walls were cracked, and Daddy covered them with old newspapers to keep the cold air out. After I learned to read, I'd go up to the wall and read those papers. I still remember a big ad for Clabber Girl baking powder and another for Mail Pouch tobacco.

Mother did laundry in a number three size tub. She had to pump the water from the well and heat it on the two-burner coal oil stove before pouring it into the tub and scrubbing the clothes on a wash board. Her hands used to get red, sore, and blistered from wringing out clothes. It was sure the whitest and prettiest wash I have ever seen.

Mother made her own soap out of lye and lard. We used that soap for everything: baths, hair, dishes, and house cleaning. We took our baths in that big tub. In the summer, Glenda and I took ours first and Lloyd and Albert next. Each of us had to pump out our own water to heat and carry to the tub.

Mother often sat in a big chair in the living room, reading her Bible by the coal oil lamp. Besides the big chair, the living room had another chair, a couch, a couple of small tables for the lamps, and the potbelly stove. There was an old rug on the floor, but it was too small to cover all of it, and the rest of the room was bare boards.

Some nights we had only enough oil for one lamp, and mother would let us use it. That left everyone else sitting in the dark, and Mother would soon holler at us to hurry up and bring the lamp back. She wanted to get back to her Bible reading. Glenda and I would play on the beds sometimes while getting down our coats, jumping up and down and rolling around. Mother would hear us laughing and yell at us to stop at once. We obeyed immediately because if she had to come in, it would be with switches, and she would whip us good.

She would tell us something only one time. The second time would get you a whipping. She was very strict with us. Sometimes Daddy would say, "Marie, lay off them girls; they are just having fun." But Mother paid no mind to him.

We didn't have any toys to play with. Glenda and I dressed up in Mother's old clothes--hat and dress and high heel shoes somebody gave her. We made a doll out of rags and pretended we were married and had a baby.

We did have a swing in the front yard and some old tires. Lloyd, Glenda, and I took turns getting inside the tires, and the others would roll us down the road. That was fun. One time Lloyd made some wooden stilts, and we learned to walk on them.

I knew Christmas only as the day that Christ was born and Easter as Passover something day. Mother told us very young that there was no Santa Claus or Easter Bunny because she knew we wouldn't be getting anything. But when Christmas came, Daddy would bring in the biggest tree he could find to put up. The only decorations were things that we kids made in school out of colored paper.

I loved that tree because it made the house smell so good. One Christmas morning I heard a noise on the porch. I opened the door and found two boxes. I ran back to the bedroom and got Mother up, and we brought the boxes in. In one small box was a chicken, some canned food and other stuff. It was a good thing because that was all we had to eat that day. The other box was full of clothes.

We learned later that someone had given our names to the Salvation Army, and they had supplied the food and clothes. For this reason, even today, I never pass up a Salvation Army bucket. I always put something in because they help the poor people, and I remember how it was with us. On other occasions, other people in the neighborhood also brought us food and clothes. Sometimes when we were given clothes, they would fit only one or two of us. Poor Glenda didn't get any because she was so tiny and skinny that nothing fit her. Mother would take some of them and make them over to fit her. Later in life, when Glenda worked in a restaurant, she bought many meals for people when they came in hungry and had no money. Somebody once gave us a big box of shoes. When I found a pair that fit, I wore them to school until they got holes in them. Then Mother would cut cardboard up and put it inside the shoes to make them last longer.

I can remember only one time that I got new shoes. It was in 1943, and I was six at the time. My brother Jimmy brought them home with him when he was on leave from the Army. There was a pair each for Glenda, Lloyd, and me. They were black and white saddle oxfords. Glenda's were too big, so Mother stuffed old socks in them so that she could wear them. Lloyd's box contained two left shoes. How we all laughed over that. I loved Jimmy. I suppose our brother Jimmy knew that we would need new shoes to start school.

We went to Hendricks Township School about eight miles from home. It had five big rooms, and my brother Lloyd and I were always in the same room. From the third grade up, there were two classes to every room. It went only to the eighth grade.

I had trouble adjusting to school. When I started school in the first grade, I would lay my head down on my desk and cry like a baby. The teacher, Mrs. Bogue had to get Norma out of class to come and talk to me. That went on for about a week until I settled in and got used to going to school and being away from Mother.

I never did like my fifth-grade teacher, Elva Kelly, who I don't think had any feelings for anyone. She embarrassed me every week over our lunch money. On Monday kids were expected to bring in money to pay for their lunches, including something extra if they wanted chocolate milk on Tuesdays and Thursdays.

I always had a note saying that we got free lunches. The teacher would go down the rows, calling kids up to pay their money. Instead of letting me bring up my note, she would say, "Ruth, no need for you to come up because you eat free and you know you don't get any chocolate milk."

That always badly embarrassed me, and the other kids would look at me as if I were trash. That hurts even today.

My cousin Tootie was my only friend at school, and she and I were always together. I don't know what I would have done without Tootie to talk to.

Lloyd was always in trouble at school, fighting, getting the paddle used on him, or having to stand in the corner facing the wall. He didn't like my fifth-grade teacher either, and he used to shoot her with paper wads and rubber bands. One time she slapped him, and he slapped her back. He was expelled for a week.

Lloyd wouldn't take anything off anybody. But a lot of times when he got in trouble for fighting, he hadn't started the fight but would still get the blame.

Louise told me that a couple of our cousins used to pick on Lloyd. One day when she and Lloyd got off the bus in Marietta, a big fight broke out.

Louise was quite a fighter herself, and when two boys got on Lloyd, she jumped in to help him. Her dress flew up, and, since she wasn't wearing any panties, her bare butt was showing. That didn't stop her, and she said they whipped them both.

As she and Lloyd were walking home, the mother of the two boys came out of the house and gave her some lip. Louise dared her to come out to the road, but the woman didn't, and Louise threw a handful of rocks at her. When we were young, everybody said that Louise was a real knockout, and she is a very beautiful lady today.

Sometimes Lloyd would get into a fight on the school bus, and the driver would put him out to walk the rest of the way home. Sometimes I would get off and walk with him.

One time the bus driver wouldn't even let him on the bus because of something he had done in school. He didn't get home until about seven, and Mother was furious at the driver. The next day Daddy and Mother went to school. When they left, they had Lloyd with them. He never went back to school and never had more than a fifth-grade education.

Glenda was a doll. We were very close, and I loved her very much. We shared everything. When Daddy did work and got paid, he would go right to town. When he came home, he would be so drunk that we didn't know how he managed to drive his old Model A. Most of the time he brought back a pint of whiskey and a case of beer but no food to feed the six or eight of us at home.

The only meal I usually got in twenty-four hours was the lunch I got at school that the county paid for. I remember coming home from school and finding nothing in the ice box but some meat drippings in a can.

Many times Mother would write a note and give it to me to take down the lane to Vera Sweets' house. When I learned to read, I discovered that Mother was begging for any kind of food that Vera could spare. Vera would put some food in a box or sack, and I would thank her. She would say, "Okay, now hurry home." She was a very kind and sweet person.

That wasn't the only place that Mother sent me. She would give me notes to take to Louise Pile and another lady named Bernice. I would hand them the notes, and they began to fill up a box or whatever they had and hand it to me. I was always polite and thanked them, happy that we would have something to eat that night. My sister Norma said she'd done that too, taken notes begging for food from Louise and Vera and our aunt Martha. During World War II there were ration stamps for some items that Mother would trade for more food.

We were related to half the people who lived in Marietta, but Mother never sent me to any of them. I was too little to be ashamed. I did only what my mother asked me to do.

Mother and Daddy were always getting into fights over his drinking. One night he came home drunk, and he and Mother got into an awful argument. The next morning she got up and put her shoes on. Her feet began to burn, and she yanked the shoes off. Daddy had poured lye in them during the night. Her feet were so badly blistered that she could hardly walk for days. He had also taken her best dress that she wore to church from behind the bedroom door and cut it to pieces.

Another night Mother got scared and took Glenda and me out of the house. She told Lloyd we would be in the church toilet and to come get us when Daddy went to bed. But when Lloyd came later, he told us that Daddy was sitting up in a chair with his shotgun and had told him he was going to kill Mother when she came home. We stayed in that old toilet all night, scared to death that Daddy would find us. It smelled so bad in there that we could hardly breathe.

We went home at dawn and found Daddy asleep. No more was ever said about it, and Daddy woke up in a good mood. Mother acted as if she had totally forgotten, but I hadn't.

Another time Lloyd, Glenda, and I were coming home on the school bus and saw Daddy beating Mother up in the ditch that ran across the gravel road to the house. We jumped out of the bus and got Daddy off of her. Her nose was bleeding, and the next day she had a black eye. Daddy had been acting that way for a long time. Erva told me about one time when Daddy was beating Mother and Erva tried to get between them. Daddy threw her across the kitchen floor. Her leg hit the table, and she received a nasty gash on the knee. She still has the scar. Another time when Daddy came in drunk, he got his shotgun and threatened to kill Mother. Albert tied him to a chair all night. And, when Mother was pregnant with Norma, Erva said Daddy gave her such a terrible beating it was a wonder that Norma survived.

I don't know why Daddy treated Mother so badly, and I have never forgiven him for it. She was a good woman and a good mother.

He didn't want her going to church. She went every Wednesday, Friday, and Sunday, taking me and Glenda with her. She was always reading her Bible and telling him that he'd better change his ways and get saved. That made him very angry, and, when he got drunk, he took it out on her.

Mother told me once that she started most of the fights with him because she was furious when he went to the taverns to drink She also accused him of going with other women.

Sometimes we would all pile in the Model A Ford and go to town with Daddy. He gave Mother money for groceries and let us off at my sister Norma's house. Norma would take Mother to the store, and Daddy would go get drunk.

By evening, Mother would have enough of waiting on him, and she would go to the tavern and drag him out. When they got home, they really had it out. Mother had a terrible temper and would tell him off. If he was in a good mood, he would just laugh at her.

Sometimes when Mother got to the tavern, he would be up on the bar dancing, and people would be throwing money at him. Other times he would be sitting with a woman and buying her drinks--while we went hungry because we didn't have any money for food.

The bar was nicknamed the Bloody Bucket because there was so much fighting. But Daddy never did any fighting there; he was having too much fun. He saved his fighting for home.

When he left the tavern, he was always broke but had a bottle in his back pocket. When he got home, he would try to hide it from Mother. If she found it, she would pour it out. Then he would go back to the tavern, climb up on the bar and dance until they threw him enough money to get another bottle.

After I grew up, people would tell me what a good dancer he was. Jerry, a woman who lived next door to me after I got married, used to work with my Daddy at a furniture factory and told me what a nice guy and good worker he was. Little did she know.

Yes, he was a good worker--when he worked. But most of the time he was just drunk.

On one of those trips to town, we had waited for him all day at my sister Norma's house. Late at night he finally came back, drunk and crazy. He beat on the doors and windows and shouted that he was going to kill Mother. Norma climbed out a window and called the police who came and hauled him off to jail. The next day, Norma and Mother got him out of jail and took him home, Mother arguing with him all the way.

If Daddy was broke, he would drink rubbing alcohol or canned heat--anything he could find. Sometimes in the summer he made watermelon or dandelion wine. That just made him silly. There were a few times when Daddy's problem was good for a laugh. One such time involved Glenda and I and a swarm of bees. Behind our house was an old, but somewhat well built tool shed. It had tools in it all right, but it also had Daddy and Gene's still and it was no real secret that Daddy and Gene had been brewing homemade beer and grape wine. It was during the duration of time that it would take for the beer and the wine to ferment that a swarm of honeybees decided that the shed would make a great place to set up housekeeping.

The shed gave the bees shade from the hot sun, the late summer rains and plenty of nourishing spirits to meet the food requirements of the bee workers and no doubt the queen bee.

No one knows and certainly not two little girls, how long the bees had been in the shed when we found them. Glenda was not afraid of the bees and was playing with them they were as drunk as drunk could be. In a drunken state the bees still knew how to sting and three of them managed enough strength to sting Glenda. I went running for Mother and she enjoyed the thrill of dumping Daddy and Gene's hidden treasure of booze. And, yes those bees had to find another home after mother got through with them. I wonder what their honey would have been like, beer, and sweet wine honey? At any rate we did have a good laugh with Mother after her extermination was completed. Daddy would turn our battery-operated radio to a country music station and dance for hours until Mother, who didn't like country music, made him turn it off.

She would say, "Hurley, if you don't turn that thing off right now, I'm going to throw it out the door."

After she fussed for awhile, he would turn it off.

Mother didn't know it, but I loved that country music coming from Nashville. I still do and watch it on TV every night now. If Daddy was home on Saturday night, Mother would let us listen to the Grand Ole Opry on the radio. Daddy and I would get up and dance flat-footed and square dancing. Oh how I enjoyed the dancing. My brother Albert would sing along. He liked Ernest Tubb and Hank Williams the best, but Daddy and I loved them all.

We didn't have many good times with Daddy, but I sure enjoyed those few times.

I loved all my brothers, but Albert was special to me. He was the oldest and the kindest and sweetest to me. He was about 6' 2", skinny, with black hair and dark eyes. He was really handsome.

He taught Glenda and me how to drive the old Model A when we were so little that we had to sit on his lap. He showed us how to keep it in the middle of the road. If another car was coming, he would take the wheel. As we got older, he taught us about shifting gears and how to use the clutch and brakes. One time he let me help him change a tire.

Albert and Lloyd worked with Daddy building fences, but, if Daddy didn't work, Albert wouldn't either. All he would do at home was lie on the couch. Daddy called Albert lazy. When I asked Mother once why

Albert wouldn't work, she told me she had a hard time giving birth to him. He weighed eleven pounds, and the doctor dropped him on his head.

Albert married a girl when he was in his forties, but that lasted less than a year. He left her and went back to live with Mother, and his wife divorced him. I never knew him to drink liquor.

My brother Jimmy died in 1944 at the age of nineteen. I was only seven at the time and had never gotten to know him very well.

I do remember the day that Lloyd, Glenda, and I were playing in the front yard when we heard someone singing "Old Rosalita," Jimmy's favorite song. I looked down the road and saw Jimmy walking along with his duffle bag on his shoulder. We ran down to see him. He tossed his duffle bag in the ditch, put Lloyd around his neck, picked up Glenda and me, and carried us home. It was the last time I ever saw him.

One day a taxi drove up to the house, and the driver handed Mother a telegram. Mother opened it and then ran into the house crying her eyes out. She cried for days at the news that Jimmy was dead.

The telegram said that he had been killed in West Virginia when he fell off a boat and drowned. Mother didn't believe that because he was such a good swimmer.

My brother Gene served in the Army in Korea during the Korean War. He was married and had two children. He was wounded, and they sent him back to the hospital at Camp Atterbury in Edinburg, Indiana.

His wife and I would go down and see him two or three times a week. I had never seen so many wounded soldiers, some of them in terrible shape. But I was a good looking gal, and, as we walked down the long hall, the soldiers would start whistling and hollering at us. I'd hear Gene say, "That must be my sister Ruthie coming."

His eyes would just light up, and he would have a big grin on his face because he was so glad to see us.

He married his first wife three times and divorced her three times.

Norma, Gene, and Louise didn't live at home when I did, and I don't remember much about them from those years. They were living with other families.

Norma has told me she lived with Louise and Fred Pile for two years, cleaning the chicken house, helping with housework, and pulling a wagon around town delivering milk while Louise was cooking and feeding line men.

Daddy made a turtle trap, and he liked to hunt rabbits, using a sawed-off double-barreled shotgun. In the winter he both hunted rabbits and set traps for them. Sometimes I would go with him when he checked the traps, carrying a sack to put the rabbits in. I didn't like the traps because the rabbits would be alive, just caught by a paw.

Daddy would knock them in the head to kill them, and I would pick them up still kicking. They were in pain and dying in my hands, and I felt sorry for them. Daddy was very careful. If there was anything about the rabbits he didn't like, he would bury them.

While I felt sorry for the rabbits, we had to eat. And they did make fine eating. Mother would fry them and make gravy out of the pan drippings. Sometimes she made rabbit stew, which we all liked.

One time Daddy brought home a great big turtle from a trap he had set down in Camp Merrys River. It was the biggest turtle any of us had ever seen, and I don't know how he got it home.

He and Albert tried to kill it, but that turtle was too big to hold on to. The way you usually killed a turtle was to tease it until it bit down on a pair of pliers, pull its head out and chop it off. A little turtle could be handled by one person, but not this monster.

Daddy told Lloyd, Glenda, and me to stand on top of it. We did, but it got right up and walked away with all three of us aboard. Albert was laughing so hard he almost wet his pants, and Daddy was getting madder and madder.

Finally he called Mother out to stand on it. When she put her 160 pounds on the turtle, it didn't walk anymore. Daddy got it to bite those pliers, and Albert chopped its head off.

Daddy used to say that a turtle had seven different kinds of meat. All I know is that it was good. Mother would do a good job cleaning the turtle meat and soak it in salt water for hours. Then she would salt and pepper it, roll it in flour, and fry it in lard in a big skillet. The meat kept moving in the skillet, and I told my mother that I wasn't going to eat anything that moves like that.

"Ruthie, that is just the muscles relaxing," she told me. "When it gets done, it won't do that."

When it was cooked, I was so hungry I didn't worry about its moving and ate it happily. It tastes like chicken. We had a lot of rabbit and turtle. In the winter, it was usually all we had, along with biscuits and gravy. My mother and daddy both cooked, and I can still smell that meat cooking and biscuits baking. I haven't eaten rabbit or turtle since I left home, and I miss it.

Chapter Two

I'll say one thing for Mother: she really taught me how to clean house. One time she told me to mop the kitchen floor. I hated to do that because the old linoleum was cracked and filled with holes, and I had to do it with a rag on my hands and knees. I wanted to go out and play, so I hurried through the job.

I went out the front door, and Mother followed me right out and told me to march right back in.

"Ruthie," she said, "do you see this little brush?" It was about the size of a toothbrush.

"Yes," I said. "You didn't do a very good job. Do you see this spot?" I looked down and saw the little spot that I had missed.

"You take this brush," she went on, "and you mop this floor over."

I must have been on my hands and knees for hours. I got bone tired, and my hands and knees hurt. But I kept at it because I knew I would get a good whipping if I didn't.

Mother finally told me I could get up and asked, "Did you learn how to mop a floor?"

I told her yes, and she let me go. But I hurt too bad to go out and play, so I went to bed instead. I was sore for days.

When I came home from school, I would be hungry but there usually wouldn't be anything to eat.

Glenda and I had to do the housework, so there would always be dishes for us to do. Glenda and I would start on the dishes, then start throwing water on each other. Whenever Mother caught us doing that, she would warn us one time to stop. We knew better than to ignore her warning. If we had run late that morning and hadn't got the coats off the bed, we would have to hang them up.

Mother didn't like flies in the house, and she would open the back door and chase them out with some rags.

One time a big rat got into the kitchen, and Daddy told Lloyd, Glenda, and me to get on top of the table. Mother got the broom, and Daddy got a big stick he kept in the house. They cornered the rat, and beat it to death.

We had a dog named Trixie that Thelma had brought home as a puppy and a big yellow tomcat called Cheche. Mother wouldn't let any animal in the house. We would sneak them in sometimes, but, when

Mother found out, the animals went out, and we got a whipping.

Mother was always baking--biscuits if we had flour, or cornbread or mush if we had corn meal. Sometimes she and Daddy picked dandelion greens all day. It would take them hours to clean them. But they made a delicious meal when she cooked them in meat drippings and served them with cornbread.

One time when Mother was teaching Glenda and me how to peel potatoes, we peeled them so thick that she made us peel the peelings.

Our mismatched plates and bowls were chipped and cracked, and we hardly had enough silverware to go around. But we always ate at the kitchen table, and I still think that is why they make them.

We didn't dare put our fingers in any food when it was ready. One time Mother had supper on the table, and I reached to get a little bit, and she caught me with my fingers in it.

"Ruthie, you put your hand on the table," she said. I did, but pulled my hand away when she tried to slap it. She hurt her hand on the table, and then I got my hand smacked good.

Other times Mother was busy making over clothes that people gave us, sewing them by hand.

Sometimes she just studied her Bible.

I hated Saturday mornings. Saturday was major cleaning day. We had to move everything and clean. We took the old rug in the living room outside and hung it over the clothes line. We beat on it with a broom until all the dirt and dust had been shaken out of it.

Before we could put the rug back, we had to sweep the wooden floor. The floor was full of cracks and hard to clean. I had learned from mopping the kitchen floor to do it right the first time. I sure didn't want to do it over again.

One time I turned the mattress over on Mother and Daddy's bed and found a bottle. I opened it, stuck my finger in and tasted it. It burned my tongue. I didn't like it. I didn't tell Mother about the bottle. I just put it back. If I had told her, she would have poured it out, and there would have been a big fight.

I had always wondered why Daddy stayed in the bedroom so much. After finding his whiskey bottle, I knew why.

One time Mother found Daddy's whiskey bottle and said she was going to break him from drinking. She poured half of it out and peed in it. When he found out what she had done, he started beating her. Albert and Lloyd had to pull him off.

"Marie, you leave my whiskey alone," he said, "or I'll kill you."

It was a good thing that some of the boys were home or Mother wouldn't have lived so long. She never did touch his booze after that.

One day Glenda and I were playing in the yard, and Mother told us to run down to Aunt Martha's and tell her to call the doctor to come fast. She thought Daddy was dying because he had drank some more canned heat.

After taking care of my father, the doctor told Mother, "Marie, if he ever drinks that stuff again, don't you call me. He deserves to die."

When I grew up, I asked her why she had put up with him. She said a lot of it was her fault because she was jealous of him and loved him so much. She laughed and said, "If I had left his whiskey alone and kept my mouth shut, Daddy probably wouldn't have laid a hand on me."

Lloyd, Glenda, and I didn't have dolls, roller skates, bicycles, or any other toys of our own. But we did have cousins who would let us play with their toys.

Our landlord Bill had a bicycle that he would let Norma, Glenda, and Lloyd ride, but not me because he didn't like me. Norma had his bike one day and told me, "Sis, meet me up on the Front Road and I'll take you for a ride."

I got on the handlebars, and we started off. She was riding fast, and, when she hit a big rock in the road, I got thrown off. I hit my head on something, and it started bleeding. That like to have scared Norma to death. She started crying and telling me she was sorry. I wasn't hurt badly although I do have a tiny scar from it. Norma wouldn't take me for any rides after that.

When Glenda had Bill's bike, I would meet her on the Front Road, and she would let me ride it.

The main road through Marietta was called Front Road, and it was paved. We lived on a gravel road. Marietta had only about four roads that went anywhere.

When I talk about uptown, I mean an area of Marietta that was only about three or four blocks from our house. There was nothing there but two grocery stores and one gas station.

There was a Methodist church in the town, and I remember going to church on Sundays and at Easter. All the girls wore pretty dresses, black patent leather shoes, and ribbons in their hair. All I had was an old hand-me-down dress and shoes with holes in them. I used to think how great it would be to look like that. The other girls would make fun of me.

Mother, Glenda, and I always sat in the front row. Mother never did want to miss anything being said. I don't think that anyone ever sat next to us. They called us dirty old Spurlins. But I was clean as a pin, and I couldn't understand why they would call me dirty. We had baths every day, and our hair was washed twice a week.

My hair was long strawberry blonde, and, when Mother washed it, it looked just like wheat and would sparkle in the sun. But I had some things the other girls didn't; I had good looks and was well built. Some people would say that Hurley Spurlin had the best looking girls around Marietta.

We might have been poor, but we were a very close-knit family and loved and were proud of each other. It is still the same way today. My sisters and other family are my friends. When I get lonely, I pick up the phone and call one of them or go home for a visit.

As the years went on, Mother and Daddy didn't do as much fighting. Mother was going through change of life and nearly bled to death a few times. She would get migraine headaches and would be in bed for three days, throwing up. We had to keep the bedroom dark as she couldn't stand the light coming in the window.

My sister Thelma had to come and take care of us kids. Thelma never had any children, but she knew how to take care of us. She was so good and loving to Glenda and me, it was like having Mother there.

Mother was in and out of the hospital in Indianapolis. During one of her hospital stays I had the chicken pox and mumps. Mother also had trouble with her throat. She couldn't swallow anything without choking, a problem she had until the day she died.

Chapter Three

When I was about nine, I took a note up to Louise Pile again begging for food. Louise lived on a farm with her husband and son. She sold eggs, milk, butter, cottage cheese, ice cream, and chickens to stores and homes in Marietta. Louise gave me some food but sent a note back with me asking Mother if I could do some work for her. I guess she got tired of giving us food for nothing. Mother told her I could. My sister Norma had worked there but had gotten married.

When I left the house for my first day working for Louise, Mother told me to mind my manners and to clean for Louise just like I cleaned at home. If I didn't, she said, I'd get a whipping. I didn't want any of her green Willow switches. They burned too bad.

I'll never forget that first day. It was summer, and the first job Louise had me do was clean her chicken house. The manure must have been three or four inches deep. She told me I had to do a good job because she had a new batch of chickens coming for the winter.

She gave me a tool that consisted of a long handle with a two-foot blade on one end. I had to bear down on the scraper with all my might as I pushed it forward. The smell was so bad that I had to go out every once in awhile to get some fresh air.

At noon she gave me a good dinner, and I went back to work. By then my arms and my stomach muscles hurt from the effort. About four o'clock she said I could go home, but, since I was no way near done, I would have to come back to finish it.

The next morning I was so sore I could hardly get out of bed. But Mother said, "Ruthie, you get right up and get down to Louise's." Mother fried me some mush, which was all there was to eat, and I walked to

Louise's, hurting with every step I took. I knocked on the door to let her know I was ready for work, and she invited me in to have some bacon and eggs and coffee. I had been raised on coffee because we didn't have any milk.

She told me not to work so hard that day and gave me a mask. The mask helped, and I thanked God for it because the smell just about made me sick. It took me a week to get that job done. Louise kept coming out and giving me cold Kool-Aid which sure tasted good on my dry throat.

When I finished that week, Louise told me I could come back on Monday to clean the milk house. I worked for Louise for about three years. I not only cleaned, but I also learned how to churn butter, clean and pluck chickens, make ice cream, and can fruits and vegetables.

When Louise was ready to can, she dug a hole, lined it with bricks, filled it with wood and started a fire. We would put a big number three tub on top of the bricks and fill it with water. We would fill canning jars with green beans or tomatoes or whatever she was canning that day and let them cook for hours. Every once in awhile we would put on more wood to keep the fire going.

The Piles were probably the first family in the area to get electricity, and they had hot and cold water and an inside bathroom. Electricity was being installed in other homes in Marietta at the time, and Louise cooked the linemen their dinner.

I never had to work in the dairy barn, but I did have to clean the milk house. I didn't like the smell in there very well, but I sure loved the cold milk, particularly on mornings when I hadn't had any breakfast. Louise frequently fixed me something to eat when I arrived, but, if she didn't, I often went hungry all morning except for the milk.

When I was done with the milk house, I would clean the main house, making beds, picking up clothes, and cleaning the bathroom. As soon as I was done with that, I had to set the long table for ten or twelve men. Fred Pile came in first and ate, then the son. They ate at a table in the sun room, and I cleaned up after them.

Then the linemen came in and had their dinner. While they were eating, I had to go back and clean the bathroom again. After that, Louise and I sat down in the sun room and had our dinner. I was always starved. Some days I didn't think I would make it through all the work, but her good food was worth waiting for.

After we finished our meal, Louise and I cleaned up and did the dishes. Then she started cooking and baking for the next day's meal. She would then give me orders on what to do next and would take an hour's nap. While she was sleeping, I would peel potatoes or break green beans and put them in water in the refrigerator, or I would sweep the floors and dust the furniture. When four o'clock came, I could go home.

I was so tired I never knew what being a kid meant. At home there were more dirty dishes waiting for me and all those old coats to hang up. There usually wasn't anything to eat except perhaps some mush or dandelion greens. Once in awhile there might be some macaroni and cheese left. But most of the time, what I ate at Louise's was all I had all day. Occasionally Louise would give me some leftovers to take home, but there were seldom leftovers.

Louise bragged about me to everyone, telling them what a good worker I was. My pay for a week's work was three or four dollars which I gave to my mother to buy food with. That amount of money went a long way then. Sometimes Louise would give me a big basket of food that she let me pull home in her son's wagon.

One week she had gone into Shelbyville to do her shopping at the big stores. At the end of the week she handed me a bag of clothes and shoes she had bought me at a rummage sale and told me that was for my week's work.

When Daddy learned about that, he got mad. He gave me a note to take to Louise the next Monday saying that I was to be paid or I couldn't work there any more. After that, Louise stopped feeding me. She told me to bring my lunch and never gave me any more leftovers to take home. Since I didn't have anything for lunch, I would drink all the milk I could and eat some of the cottage cheese in the coolers in the milk house.

The linemen finished their work, and Louise told me that she didn't need me any more. It was the end of summer, and school was starting. I still had my work at home to do after school every night. We were still using coal oil lamps as we were the only family still without electricity.

That winter, Louise got sick, and I went back to work for her three or four days a week. In the beginning, I loaded up a little red wagon and tugged it through the snow, delivering milk and eggs before school. The wagon was hard to pull though the snow; it was cold, and I was scared.

After a short time, Louise began delivering the milk and eggs in her car, and I cleaned her house or did whatever else she wanted done. And I continued to collect three to four dollars for my week's work which I gave to my mother.

As part of spring cleaning, Louise and I tore off her wall paper and hung new paper. We worked quite well together. She cut it, and I would paste it and help her hang it. After that we washed the woodwork and then painted it. I worked for her for two or three hours after school and all day on Saturdays.

I could finally relax when I was home and could watch from across our street the field full of milk cows   owned by a woman named Ellen Blocher. Glenda and I would watch her as she milked the cows in the barn, and we would play on an old piano she had stored there.

We saw a lot of calves being born there, and I thought that was neat. But I couldn't understand why the mother cow dropped her baby on the ground like that. I thought it must really hurt, and I didn't like that   One day our neighbor across the street, a hair dresser named Alice Blocher, a sister in-law of Ellen Blocher asked mother if I could clean her house on Saturdays. Alice and her husband had no kids, and I was always done by noon. The first time I cleaned for her there was a lot of change lying on her dresser. It took me awhile to pick it all up and drop it in a big glass jar so that I could dust the dresser.

Alice came over to our house and told Mother what a good job I had done. She paid Mother five dollars and told me that from then on I could have all the change I found there. Mother told her no I couldn't.

"She isn't allowed to take anything that doesn't belong to her. She knows she would get a whipping. You paid her for her work." My mother taught me not to lie, cheat, or steal. I'm grateful for the morals she taught me.

The next Saturday Alice gave me a note asking Mother if she could give Glenda and me a permanent. While she did Glenda's hair, I cleaned the house. Then she did my hair and gave me five dollars. I really loved Alice.

Lloyd also did odd jobs, and in the summer he would help the farmers de-tassel the corn. He also helped our landlord Bill haul trash for the neighbors. He gave his money to Mother too.

There just wasn't enough food for all of us, though, and Mother sent Glenda to live with a family named Shoemore for awhile. I'll never forget the day they came to pick her up. Glenda was crying and waving goodbye to us as the car pulled away, and Mother and I were crying just as hard. We didn't stop crying for days.

Mother couldn't get rid of me because I refused to go with anyone. Besides, nobody wanted me; they all wanted Glenda.

One day Mrs. Shoemore asked if they could adopt Glenda, but Mother said no. I don't have any idea how long Glenda stayed with them. All I know is that I missed her. The day that the Shoemores brought her home, Lloyd and I were playing with the old tires, rolling each other over and over in them. Glenda jumped out of the car and hopped down the road after us. She could hardly walk because she had a big boil on her leg. We hugged and kissed her and rolled her in the tire.

She came back with a lot of new clothes and new shoes. When we went to Sunday school, she was all dressed up while I still had my old dress and shoes filled with holes. But I didn't care because I was so happy that we had Glenda back again. I remember when Glenda, Tootie and I were walking through an alley past the house of one of our cousins, she called us a nasty name and I jumped the fence, grabbed her, shoved her in the old toilet, and locked the door. As I left, she was yelling for her mother to come let her out.

Chapter Four

When I was about twelve, Glenda left us again when Mother had to go to Franklin, Indiana, to take care of her father who was then ninety-eight. Daddy took Mother and me over to Franklin, and Glenda went to live with Mrs. Bogue, our first grade teacher. Mrs. Bogue used to bring Glenda to Franklin every two weeks to see us.

That was the first I remember seeing much of my grandfather. I called him Grandpa Kerr; Mother called him James A. He had been blind for years by that time. About all I knew about him was that he loved doughnuts, hot dogs, and bananas.

I don't think he liked me. I know his wife Anne didn't like me at all because I had always refused to sit on her lap and let her kiss me. I didn't know her, and I wasn't about to sit on any stranger's lap. She did love Glenda and Lloyd and was always giving them chewing gum and candy. I didn't get any, apparently because of my refusal to sit on her lap.

Lloyd wouldn't share his gum and candy with me, but Glenda and I would go outside where she shared hers.

When we arrived in Franklin, Anne was in the hospital. I don't know what happened to her. She never came back to the house, and I never saw her again.

Grandpa Kerr's house had three rooms and a large porch. There was electricity but no running water in the house, and the toilet was outside.

While Mother was taking care of Grandpa, she slept on a half bed across from his. I slept on the couch in the living room but kept my clothes in Grandpa's room along with Mother's.

Grandpa never wanted me in his bedroom. If he was sitting in the living room and I started across the floor for something, he would shake

25

his cane at me and demand to know where I was going. He may have been blind, but his hearing was quite good.

I came home from school one day, and he was sitting in the living room, chewing tobacco and spitting into an old coffee can.

"It's me, Grandpa," I said as I came in. "Where is Mother?"

"She went to the store. You sit on that couch and don't move."

Mother always made me change clothes when I came home from school, so I decided to crawl into the bedroom to get my clothes. I was almost in the bedroom when he came at me with that cane. I was barely staying out of his way when Mother came in.

"James A., don't you hit her," she said to him, then asked me, "Ruthie, what were you going in there for?"

When I told her I just wanted to change my clothes, Grandpa said, "From now on, Marie will get your clothes for you. Don't you ever go in there again."

One day I found out why he didn't want me in there.

One of Anne's daughters came by, and he and Mother were going through the trunk. Mother was counting out some money. When she was done, Grandpa gave half of it to Anne's daughter.

After she left, Mother told me that Grandpa had a lot of money in the trunk, and he thought I might steal it. I never went into his bedroom after that.

One night Mother and I had just stepped up on the porch coming back from church when Grandpa threw tobacco juice all over our coats. That got Mother mad.

"James A.," she said, "you be more careful where you throw that stuff and make sure nobody is around!"

Not too long after that, Grandpa got sick. Mother had to put him in the hospital, where he died. In his will, he had left his house and money to Mother, but he had been living on welfare, and the welfare people came and took everything. Mother got nothing.

After Grandpa died, Daddy came and picked us up. On our way home, we stopped at school and got Glenda. It was the last time she had to live with anyone else.

Daddy always kept pickles in salt brine in the back room. One day I came home from school and went to get a pickle out of the barrel. When I turned around, I discovered that we had a new washing machine that ran on gasoline.   On Saturdays, Glenda, Lloyd, and I would have to pump water for the washing machine and then heat it up. Then we pumped water to fill the number three tub for rinsing.

The washer was started with a crank that took a lot of effort. One time we watched as Mother tried to start the washer by pushing down on the crank with her foot. Her foot slipped and she nearly broke it. She could hardly walk for days.

Lloyd got it started, and I started to wring out the clothes with the hand-cranked wringer. I did fine for awhile, but then I got my hand caught. None of us knew how to release it, and I began screaming for Mother. Daddy came out and shut it off and got my hand out.

Poor Mother and Daddy had to finish the wash. The next day Mother couldn't walk, and my hand was sore, swollen, and black and blue. I couldn't use my fingers, and I didn't go to school for almost a week.

Mother never did try starting that thing again, leaving it to the boys or Daddy, but I learned to handle the wringer very well.

As he got older, Daddy stopped drinking as much as he had. He was getting quite sick at times.

One time he got a job setting out tomato plants for a farmer. It was a big field to plant, and Mother, Lloyd, Albert, Glenda, and I helped. We nearly broke our backs, but we got the job done.

We always had a nice yard. Our landlord, Bill, did the mowing. In the spring he would get Mother flower seeds. How Mother loved her flowers. She planted them in the spring, and by summer the garden would be blooming. Then disaster struck.

We had a nanny goat that Daddy milked. He used to sell the milk to the preacher who had a baby that required goat milk. One day the goat chewed through the rope and wandered to a neighbor's house where it dirtied all over her porch. The neighbor woman came down the road with that goat screaming, "Marie, you get out here and get this goat. And then you clean up its mess."

Mother got mad and grabbed the big stick Daddy kept in the house and went after the neighbor. The woman turned and started running, and Mother chased her all the way home, shouting, "If I get a hold of you I'll give you a beating you won't forget. And I'm not going to clean up any mess." She didn't, either.

After that, Daddy sold the goat to the preacher. That woman and my mother remained friends. She was probably afraid not to be. That goat constantly tried eating the flowers in mother's flower garden and was a constant pest until Daddy got rid of it.

We had a playful dog named Trixie. He would chase us around the flower garden, pass us up, then let us pass him. He played ball with us and hide and seek. We loved that dog and had more fun with him. But he had to stay outside, and one winter he froze to death, I think Mother said. That hurt us all.

Chapter Five

Sometimes we would stay with Aunt Daisy in Franklin for a couple of days at a time. We had a good time with her, and I loved her. She was a good cook, and we ate well there. She could really play a piano, and she would play and sing along with us. All she played were Christian songs, but I enjoyed them.

Aunt Gertie lived in California with her two daughters and one son. I saw her only two or three times in my life. But she sent big boxes of clothes, including shorts and long pants, and shoes, nail polish, makeup, and perfume.

We girls weren't allowed to wear makeup, nail polish, shorts, or long pants, so that all ended up in the trash. We did get to keep the perfume. A deck of cards Aunt Gertie once sent went into the fire because we weren't allowed to play with any cards.

Mother wrote Aunt Gertie and told her not to send any more makeup, nail polish, pants, or shorts to us girls. But when I opened another box from Aunt Gertie later, I found a little box of makeup and nail polish on top. I took the box out fast, and Mother didn't know that Aunt Gertie had sent it until she caught me wearing it one day. Then I had to tell her what I had done. It all went into the trash, and that was the end of that.

My Grandpa Spurlin lived in Shelbyville. I don't remember seeing him more than two or three times. My sister Erva said Grandma and Grandpa Spurlin were really good to Mother and she really loved them. Erva said they all would have starved if it weren't for Grandma and Grandpa. I wish they had lived long enough for me to know them. I miss not having had any grandmothers to talk to or share secrets with. But I had plenty of sisters and a good mother, so I'm pretty lucky. Grandpa Spurlin fell and broke his hip and was hospitalized. When he got out, they brought him to our house in a hospital bed and put him in our only bedroom. Mother took care of him for about six weeks.

The night before he died, he called Lloyd, Glenda, and me into the bedroom and told us never to mistreat Mother. He said she had always been a good woman and a beautiful person.

He died about six the next morning. I won't ever forget that day.

Nor will I ever forget the day of his funeral. Daddy was sitting on the end of the front row at the funeral home, drunk as a monkey. He fell off the chair, embarrassing us all. Lloyd and Albert had to pick him up and sit by him to prop him up.

On Daddy's side of the family were Aunt Della, Uncle Charlie Tucker, and Aunt Eddie. Uncle Charlie and Aunt Eddie were my Grandma Spurlin's brother and sister, which made them my great uncle and great aunt. Daddy's sister, Aunt Edith, had six children, one son being Earl Wayne, who we played with and fought with a lot. On one occasion he shot me with a sling shot in between my breasts with a rock and I have a scar from it today. I did have a nice bust, and Earl Wayne always called me the sweater girl. My aunt Edith was a very pretty lady. She died very young.

I think of them often. I loved them dearly and know they loved and cared about us.

When Glenda and I were hungry, we would go down to Aunt Della's. She had a big family, and her house was always filled with children and grandchildren. She was a very big heavyset woman who could hardly walk.

When she saw Glenda and me in the yard, she'd say, "You two get right in here."

We would enter shyly, and she would waddle over and hand us huge plates of food. We would take our plates outside and sit on the porch. We would hear her grandkids laughing about our clothes, our shoes, and the fact that we were always hungry when we came by. Aunt Dela would tell them to shut up and not make fun of us because we had feelings too. She always treated us like family and gave us food to take home.

They were good to Daddy too. He would go down and help Uncle Charlie butcher hogs and clean chickens, and they would give him meat and food to take home. Hogs were killed in the late fall and winter, and Daddy helped several farmers in their butchering, particularly a man named Creek. He also helped kill chickens. The farmers gave him meat, and that helped keep us from going hungry in the winter.

My Daddy's Aunt Eddie had two houses. Her son and his family lived in the front house, and she lived in the back. She had a basement where she kept her canned goods and a smoke house full of meat.

Her son and his wife had eight children. My favorite cousin, whom we all called Tootie, was one of them. We were close friends, and I would often go to her house to play.

When I played with my favorite cousin Tootie, I would always get a sandwich and a glass of Kool-Aid.

Behind my Aunt Eddie's house was a big steep hill going straight down. It was covered with trees. Whenever it snowed hard enough, Glenda, Lloyd, Tootie, her brother, Glen and I would get an old piece of tin or anything we could sit on and go sliding down that hill. We would play for hours.

One time Lloyd slid into a big tree and knocked himself out. Tootie and I rubbed snow in his face, and he came around. He had a big bruise on his head the next day.

Glenda and I would usually go down together. One time she fell off halfway down the hill, and she rolled over and over, laughing all the time. Those were the good old days.   Sometimes when we were playing, Aunt Eddie would call me in the house and ask me to go down to the basement and bring up some canned goods. One time when I went down, I saw a big long black snake lying on top of the canned goods and immediately ran back up the stairs, screaming.

"Well, honey," Aunt Eddie said calmly, "just get the broom and chase it away. It won't hurt you. It lives down there."

I did what she said, gingerly poking at the snake with the broom until it just disappeared. I got the food and flew up the stairs.

"Honey, have you eaten today?" Aunt Eddie asked me. When I told her no, she fixed me up a plate of food. While I was eating, she packed a big box of food for me to take home. It was too heavy for me to carry, and I had to borrow one of the kids' wagons to pull it with. There was enough food in there, including some meat, to feed us for three or four days.

When one of us kids caught a cold, Mother would put Vicks VapoRub on our chests and cover it with a rag. Sometimes she used a garlic and mustard paste on our chests, and we seemed to get better in no time when she used that remedy. I think it was the smell that cured us.

If we stepped on a rusty nail or cut our foot, she would put a piece of meat fat on it, and it would heal in no time, scarcely leaving a scar.

I do have a pretty big scar on the bottom of one foot, though, the reminder of a wound I got when I jumped off the roof of the toilet and landed on a piece of glass.

We used a Sears catalog that we picked up somewhere as toilet paper.

Lloyd was always tormenting and teasing me and Glenda. He got the biggest kick out of scaring me to death. For example, since I was afraid of snakes, worms, and bugs, Lloyd would cut out pictures of them every chance he got and chase me with them. I would go into fits.

We had a swing between the two trees in the front yard. Another of his favorite tricks was to sit in one of the trees when Glenda and I were in the swing and spit down on us. Other times he would get behind the swing and pull our long hair. We would yell for Mother to stop him. She'd come out with a switch, and Lloyd would run for his dear life.

I was climbing the tree one day when I saw a paper sack filled with candy and gum hanging from a branch. Glenda and I ate it. When our sister Louise came home, she wanted to know who took her candy. When I admitted that I had, she chased me all over the yard and warned me never to take anything of hers again. Eventually she quit chasing me, and all was forgotten.

Glenda and I sometimes played in the old house that my Grandpa Spurlin had once owned and in which I had been born. My sisters Erva and Thelma remembered scrubbing the old floors in that house just the same as I did until it finally fell in because Daddy wouldn't fix it up. Then we moved into our landlord Bill's tar paper house. Erva never lived there herself but did come back for visits. As a matter of fact, Glenda was born in Erva's house, and one time Mother got sick and couldn't nurse Glenda. Erva had a new baby at the time, so she nursed Glenda and her baby until Mother got better. Erva said she loved to be with Mother. They would cook and bake homemade bread and pick greens. They had a good time. One day when we were playing at Grandpa Spurlin's old house, Glenda and I found some of our sister Louise's cigarettes hidden behind some torn paper on the wall. Glenda and I lit them up and tried to smoke. Lloyd found us and started for home to tell Mother. When Mother arrived, she was carrying willow switches which she used to whip us all the way home.

Actually, I got most of the whipping because I couldn't run as fast as Glenda. Other times when Glenda and I got into trouble and Mother came after us, I stayed, but Glenda ran. Then I would get it twice as hard because Mother would be mad at Glenda for running.

I don't think Louise ever found out who took her cigarettes. We girls get together now and have a ball laughing about things that happened back then.

Chapter Six

I never got to know my oldest sister, Erva, as well as I would have liked to. She was the oldest and was married and had five children of her own when I was growing up. I do remember going to her home in Shelbyville and playing with her kids.

When Norma got out of school, she went to work at a restaurant in Shelbyville. She would walk up the road to catch the bus into town. Even though she came in late, we would wait up for her because she would bring home leftovers for us. She surely did save us from going to bed hungry many a night.

Norma started dating a boy we called Junior. When Junior asked Daddy and Mother if he could marry Norma, they gave their permission. She was fourteen. Norma was really pretty with her round face and brown hair and eyes.

I loved Junior. He loved Norma and was good to her. He was also good with us kids. He would play tag with us and swim with us. He was like another brother to me.

The night before Christmas the first year they were married, she came by with candy and apples and oranges. She had presents for all of us. I was eight years old, and it was the first time Glenda, Lloyd, or I had ever gotten a present for Christmas. I don't remember what she got us, but it was probably new clothes. At Easter she came with the biggest Easter baskets she could find.

Gene and his first wife would bring us things too.

But it was when Louise got married at fifteen that things really got better at home. I don't think we went hungry anymore after Norma, Louise, and Gene got married. We also had good clothes and shoes to wear to school. I even remember Mother's getting Glenda and me a twirling baton one time, although I never did have a baby doll.

Norma, Louise, and Gene all had children by then, and they kept coming. From then on I would spend summers at one of their homes.

When I was twelve, I went to visit Gene and his wife. One day they took me to the fair, and Gene's wife put me on the merry-go-round. She had bought me some new underpants that tied on each side. When she took me off the merry-go-round, my underpants fell down. She told me to keep walking, and she picked them up and took me to the bathroom where I put them back on.

When I was thirteen, I was spending the summer with Louise. I woke up one morning with something in my panties. I thought I had an accident in my sleep. I cleaned myself up, but in no time I was a mess again. I got scared and told Louise something was wrong with me, and I showed her.

"Ruth," she said, "you've started your period."

I didn't know what she meant. She told me I would do that every month for a long time to come. My first period was painful, and I was sick all the way through it. Later, Mother would make me ginger tea when I had cramps, and that helped.

Mother hadn't told us girls anything about periods or sex. It was just never talked about. The only thing she had ever told me was to never let any man touch me "down there" because that was dirty and nasty.

Louise's husband worked on a farm, and I spent a lot of time with her. They had two boys. The second child had something wrong with him, and Louise spent most of her time holding and rocking him. She couldn't lay him down for long, so I cleaned and cooked, looked after the older boy, and rocked the baby so that Louise could get some rest. The baby died at nineteen months.

While I was living with Louise, I met a boy I liked very much, but he was killed in a motorcycle accident.

Louise's husband and I had heated a tub of water on the stove for washing one day. It was heavy, and, while we were lifting it off the stove, I let my end down too fast, and he sloshed boiling water down my leg. We put cold water on it for hours. I still have scars from those burns.

Norma kept her house very clean. She had two girls at the time, and she was strict with them. I did a lot of baby sitting while I was there because Norma worked at a factory in Shelbyville. I gave them their baths and combed their hair. I enjoyed that. Norma always checked the girls over to make sure I had cleaned them well. I also helped Norma do dishes and make beds.

One time when I was with Norma and Junior, we went to visit with his brother who had a son named Rex who was about eighteen at the time. Rex had a girlfriend named Beth and a friend named Phil who I thought was quite cute. Phil was about sixteen, and I was thirteen at the time.

Beth and I became good friends, and we spent a lot of time together. Phil came over, and we all got to talking. Phil and I started to like each other. After that, I didn't want to go anywhere but Norma's house. Every Friday night after school, Norma and Junior came down to Marietta and took me home with them.

Junior was a lot of fun. He and I would do dishes. I washed, and he dried. If he was working on his car, he'd ask me to hand him tools. But I didn't know one tool from the next. I would hand him the wrong one, and he would come out from under the car and say, "Now, Ruthie, this is the `so and so' tool; this is what I wanted. Now don't forget next time," Junior was always working on something.

One time Norma was sick on Thanksgiving Day, and Junior and I baked our first turkey together and made the whole dinner. It really was good. I will never forget the good old days with Norma and Junior. He's special.

While I was there, I went over to see Beth and Rex. Phil and I would take walks and just talk. I wasn't allowed too far out of Norma's sight. Sometimes I had her two girls with me.

Phil was my first real boyfriend. When I told Mother and Daddy I had a boyfriend and that Phil wanted to come down to Marietta and see me as soon as he got his car, Mother laid down some rules. He could come only on Saturday afternoons; I had to have my housework done; I wouldn't be allowed out of the front yard; and Glenda and Lloyd had to be out there too.

When I told Phil that, he said that was all right. He was getting his car that week and would be down that Saturday afternoon. I got my housework done by noon, and by one o'clock he was there. We sat in the swing, and Glenda and Lloyd played in the yard watching us all the time.

Mother told him that as long as he did what he was told, he could come back and I could see him from one to four on Saturdays. The next Saturday I got up late and didn't have my housework done by the time he arrived. Mother went out and told him I couldn't come out until I was finished, and he sat in the swing with Lloyd until two when I was finally done.

Phil started writing me letters, and I would get one every Wednesday. The next day in school Tootie and I would sit on top of the bleachers and talk about our boyfriends.

Norma and Junior bought their first house. They came down the Friday night before the Saturday they were to move in and asked Mother if I could go home with them. When we arrived at the house, Phil was in the back alley and came in to see me briefly. I discovered later that he lived only five houses away.

I didn't get to spend any time with Phil that weekend as I was too busy taking care of Norma's kids while they unpacked and got settled in. But Phil would drive up and down the street waving at me.

I was at Norma's the next weekend, and he came over Saturday afternoon and asked if I could go down to his house so he could show me something. Norma told him she wanted to write a note to his mother to be sure that it was all right. He took the note home and a short time later came back with his mother.

"Mom, this my girlfriend, Ruth," he said.

"My name is Bess," she told me, and we began talking.

I loved her at once, and so did Norma.

We all went back to their house, and Phil showed me some of the things he had--a movie camera, a guitar and a Hawaiian guitar, and a ukulele. He showed me some of the movies he had taken.

Phil had two brothers, Jed and Lou, and a sister named Jenny who was married to a policeman. Phil's brothers and sister were a lot older than he was. His sister was thirteen when he was born and his brothers older than that.   Phil was the spoiled one. His father, Fred Willis, didn't say much; he just looked at me. His father had a fiddle and was quite good. Phil also painted, and Bess proudly showed me a number of his paintings.

She served us a piece of homemade peach cobbler and let me have a cup of coffee.

After that, Phil came over to Norma's a lot. He would play his guitar for us. Norma was just as strict as Mother with me, and somebody was always around when we were together keeping an eagle eye on us.

Phil had a good friend, Ben, a sweet boy who was quite good looking. He was tall with dark hair and brown eyes. He had a glass eye he never wanted anyone to know about.

One afternoon, Phil, Ben, and I went swimming in the Big Blue river at Camp Merry along with Mother, Glenda, and Lloyd. Mother spent most of her time picking blackberries which grew wild all over the place.

Ben realized that his glass eye had fallen out, and we all began hunting for it. Ben found it himself and was badly embarrassed. Lloyd started laughing, and Mother slapped him good.

One weekend I wasn't expecting Phil because he had written me a letter telling me his car had broken down and he had to work on it. I had just settled into the swing when I heard voices.

I looked down the road and saw Phil and Ben on bicycles. They had ridden ten miles to see me, and were they bushed.

The following weekend, Norma let me go to the movies with Phil, Ben, Beth, and Rex. I sat between Phil and Ben. Phil and I were holding hands. Ben asked him if he could hold my other hand. Phil told him he could as long as he knew that I was his girl.

I sat through the rest of the movie holding both their hands. They were both perfect gentlemen. Later we all went to Hooks Drug Store and had fountain Cokes. For a long time it was Phil and Ben and I.

Another time Phil's car had broken down again, and his sister Jenny and her husband, Bob, offered to drive me home on Sunday. Phil and I got to sit in the back seat together, and he put his arm around me. We had known each other almost a year.

Jenny told Mother she hoped it had been all right to bring Phil along. Mother said that as long as she and her husband had both been along she guessed it was all right.

One weekend Phil, Beth, Rex, and I went roller skating at Taylor's Roller Rink. It started raining on the way home, and, since the glass in Phil's car was broken out on my side, I got soaked. I was sick with a cold all that week.

School got out in May. On July 9th I celebrated my fourteenth birthday. Phil turned seventeen on July 18.

That summer I stayed with Louise. Phil came to see me there. Louise wasn't as strict with me as Norma was, and Phil and I had a lot of good times together. But, of course, we were never left alone.

We went places together, but mostly we sat around and talked and laughed. Phil brought his guitar and played for us. His favorite song was "Blueberry Hill." He didn't like country music, and I didn't like his favorite music--classical. But that was all right with me as it was about the only thing we disagreed about.

One day that summer Mother let Phil and me sit in the car out in front of the house. Lloyd, who had been sitting in the back seat, went in the house and told Mother that Phil was playing with my breast. He was lying, but Mother came out there with her switch, dragged me out of the car, and whipped me all the way to the house. She told Phil to go home.

After I got my whipping, however, Lloyd began laughing and admitted that he had been lying. Mother then whipped him, and he didn't tell any more lies about me.

In August Phil asked me to marry him. I told him, "yes" with all the enthusiasm a girl of fourteen could summon, but I told him he would have to ask my parents for permission. He was afraid of my mother and I was too. When she got on the warpath, there was no telling what she could do. I remember that my mother and father were sitting at the kitchen table when Phil made his entrance to ask them for my hand in marriage. Daddy acknowledged that we had been going together for over a year and that it would be impossible to keep us apart much longer. My mother sat quietly for several minutes then she blurted out "yes" as she rose and went to her bedroom.

My mother knew that a new life with a husband would or could naturally be better for me, after all her other daughters, for the most part, had been happier after they had left home to build their own little nests. But, somehow I just knew she was especially sad for me that day.

The wedding was to be on September the fifteenth, 1951 but it was not to happen until I had the experience of one more beating. Age fourteen and ready to get married I was enticed to smoke a cigarette. My father caught both Glenda and I smoking and immediately told my mother who came after me for the last time with her "switch". September fourteenth, the day before I was to be married I had welts all over my legs and butt.

****

On the morning of the fifteenth day of September we gathered at my parent's home in Marrietta. We had a long drive to Kentucky where we could be married. I was dressed in some old long dress, white socks and black shoes. My hair was beautifully done and I had no makeup on. My mother brushed my hair out just before Phil came to get me. We were to be married without wedding rings, I was a virgin, it was a marriage of convenience..

We all piled into a used 48 Ford sedan for our trip to what I dreamed would be marital bliss, my mother, Phil, Bud, Joanne and myself. I will never forget that my mother let me lie about my age, I went from fourteen to eighteen within a very few minutes. Out of the corner of my eye I could see that my mother was crying as I said "I do". I turned immediately after saying "yes" and could see that her tears had not subsided, in-fact she had completely turned toward the wall, buried her face in her hands and wept.

We became a Mr. and Mrs. And left for our trip back to Marietta, Indiana I held my mother's hand and she kept right on crying. Instead of snuggling up next to my new husband I melted into my mother's tear dampened arms. Phil was silent and so were the two strangers that sat in the front seat. One of the saddest and joyless days of my life, a day that was to suppose to be filled with laughter and light hearted memories would soon be over, I hoped.

When we got back to Marietta and drove to my mother's house, we pulled into the front yard, Mother turned, took my face in hands and tenderly spoke these words; "I did this Ruthie so that you can have a better life." Kissed me and left. I watched her walk to the house, open the door and she disappeared. My Daddy's words were still all to present in my mind, "if she is old enough to bleed , she is old enough to be married.

Chapter Seven

I didn't know where we were going to live. I hadn't even thought about it. Our friends had a two-bedroom apartment, and they took us there. Phil had one of the bedrooms all fixed up and had painted a sign for the door that said "Do Not Disturb." I had no idea what the sign meant.

I knew nothing at all about sex. At bedtime I went into the bathroom to put on my gown. Phil tried to get in, but I had locked the door because I didn't want him to see those welts on my butt and legs, nor did I want him to see me naked. I hadn't been raised that way.

At my insistence, Phil agreed to get in bed. I turned the light out and slipped into my side of the bed. I had never been in bed with a man before and had no idea about what I was supposed to do. Besides that, my butt and legs were still hurting.

We tried to make love, but we both got scared. I finally showed him my welts, and he said he had wondered why I kept complaining about being sore.

I didn't want to leave the room after that, so I asked my girlfriend to come in. We had a long talk, and she explained some of the facts of life to me.

A week later I saw Mother and asked her why she hadn't told me what I was in for on my wedding night. She said she hadn't wanted me to get into trouble or pregnant before I was married.

It was awhile before we tried to have sex again. I thought it was dirty and nasty and that I was a bad girl when I did it. I couldn't enjoy sex for a long time. I talked to my sisters a lot, and they were a big help.

We didn't live with our friends very long. We got a house trailer of our own in a trailer park.

Phil had a friend named Chuck who was married and had eight children. When we went to visit him, Phil would take his guitar, and he and Chuck would sing and play their guitars for hours while I had a good time with the children.

The only thing I didn't like about it was that Phil would have a few drinks. But I didn't say anything as long as he didn't get drunk.

We had a lot of fun in those early years.

We would go roller skating with our friends and go to the movies. At one point, Phil bought an old car with a rumble seat in the back, and Phil and I and Rex and Beth would take turns riding in the rumble seat all over town.

Phil made a big sled that he would attach to the car after a good snow, and we all took turns sliding up and down the streets. We would have a ball on the sled then go to Hooks Drug Store and have fountain Cokes and French fries while we listened to music.

I loved Phil and was very jealous of him. I would give dirty looks to any girl that looked at him.

Phil and Rex loved to go coon hunting. They would take Beth and me along to shine the big spotlights up in the trees whenever they spotted a coon. They shot the coons, skinned them, and sold the hides. Sometimes we would go along the railroad tracks so that they could shoot rabbits to give to Norma.

The first Christmas after we were married, Phil and I got Glenda an accordion. She really enjoyed it and spent many hours learning how to play it. Later she taught herself to play a guitar, and she began writing songs and poetry. She is very good at it.

When I turned fifteen, I tried to get a job in a factory where my sister Norma worked but was told that I needed a work permit and had to be sixteen to get it. I went to the agency that gave out work permits and told a man there that, even though I wasn't sixteen, I was married and needed a job badly. He told me he would give me my permit but I wasn't ever to tell anyone what he had done because he could lose his job. I thanked him.

I took my work permit to the factory the next day, and they hired me to work on the paste tables where Norma worked. We were making shrouds to put on dead people at a mortuary.

One morning several months later the paste made me sick, and I ran to the bathroom, throwing up all the way. I was so sick I had to go home.

The next morning I was sick again, and I discovered that I was pregnant. I had morning sickness for all nine months.

I turned sixteen in July. I went into labor the morning of October 4 and was admitted to the hospital. I started hemorrhaging that night. They gave me straps to pull on when I was in pain. By the next morning I was so weak that I couldn't pull on the straps anymore.

The shift changed at three p.m., and a new nurse came in, took one look at my chart, and said, "Honey, you can't have this baby naturally."

She told me that my doctor was a Catholic and believed only in natural childbirth so that I needed another doctor.

"You are going to have your baby if I have to deliver it myself, or we are going to lose you and the baby."

She went out of the room and returned in no time at all to tell me I was going to the delivery room. She told me my doctor would put me under and another doctor would handle the delivery.

My doctor walked in then and calmly said, "Hi, Ruth." I told him if the baby died, I would sue him.

They took my baby with instruments, and she was born at five p.m.

October 5, 1953. She was five pounds ten ounces and was eighteen inches long. I'll never forget the moment when I came to and they told me I had my first real live baby doll.

But I didn't get to see her or hold her for several days.

I developed milk fever and became unconscious. I needed three pints of blood. I woke up once and discovered both of my arms strapped down to boards. I was getting blood in one arm and an intravenous needle in the other. I passed out again.

If it hadn't been for my mother, I would have died as they were giving me the wrong blood.

I finally woke up one morning and heard the birds chirping outside my window. But, when I opened my eyes, I couldn't see a thing. Everything was black. I heard Phil say, "I don't think she is going to make it." Mother answered from the other side of the bed, "Oh yes she is. God is taking care of that."

I was blind for a few hours, but my sight came back.

When I could see again and was fully awake, I said, "Hi, what's going on?"

I asked Phil if he had seen the baby, and he said yes, that she was a week old now and doing fine. The nurse came in and asked me if I wanted to see my baby. I said yes, and she brought her in wrapped in a little pink blanket.

I took one look at her and started to cry. I almost hadn't lived to see that beautiful little baby doll, but now she was all mine. I couldn't hold her because of all the needles in me and because I was so weak.

I said, "Mother, you prayed for us, didn't you?"

"Sure I did," she answered, "but God took care of the rest."

I asked Phil if he had given her the name I picked out for her, Lynn, and he said he had.

We were released a few days later, and an ambulance took us to the home of Phil's parents because the doctor had told Phil that I was still weak and would need help with the baby.

Phil's parents had a four-room house. The kitchen was long and so narrow that we couldn't eat in it. The other rooms were pretty big, and there was a bathroom with a shower.

We used part of the living room for a bedroom. Phil put up a folding-wall as a privacy screen around our bed at night and took it down in the morning.

After we moved in, they bought a washing machine.

I was a very good mother. I didn't want to lay Lynn down at all and held her most of the time. I would dress her in pretty little dresses, hats, and sweaters.

One warm day when she was about one month old, I decided to take a walk and show her off. I started with all the neighbors first, and they all thought she was a doll.

Then I took her over to Beth's and Rex's house. Beth wanted a baby of her own and held Lynn for awhile. Lynn fell asleep, and I put her down on Beth's bed. I sat with Beth at the kitchen table, and we had pie and coffee before I went home.

I had no sooner walked in the door when the phone rang. I picked it up, and Beth asked me, "Forget something?"

"Oh, my God," I said, "I forgot my baby!"

I hurried over to pick her up, thinking all the way that I must be a bad mother to forget my new baby.

One day when Phil came home at noon from the factory where he worked for his dinner, he brought three or four women to see our baby. They passed her around, and I didn't like that much. But I didn't want to hurt their feelings, particularly since some of them had donated blood for me.

Lynn was a good baby and never gave me any trouble. She could stand alone at six months and refused to take any more bottles, so I put her on baby food. She hated milk. She walked at nine months.

She was never spoiled even though someone had her all the time. If not me, then her grandma and grandpa or her daddy. Phil used to take her for rides in his car every night. He would put her in the steering wheel, and she loved going back and forth in it. She would fall asleep there just as she did when we were pushing her in her stroller.

Phil's sister Jenny would come over and hold Lynn for hours. Her Uncle Bob would walk around holding Lynn and teach her new words. Once he told her to say "kitty cat," and she said "kitty cot." He got the biggest kick out of that.

Chapter Eight

When Lynn was only three months old, I became pregnant again. Some time after that Beth and I had gone to the movies. A young boy came in and sat down on the other side of me. Phil came in and grabbed me and took me home.

As soon as we got in the house, he started slapping and hitting me. He told his parents that I was at the movies with some boy and they were to stay out of it.

"That isn't true, and he knows it," I said. "I have no control over who sits where in the movies. Beth will tell you that the boy didn't say a word to me."

I was frightened and shocked. I picked up my baby and went to Norma's house. I told her what had happened and asked if she would take us down to Marietta to Daddy and Mother.

We had been home for about a week when Phil showed up with his parents. He asked me to forgive him and promised never to hit me again.

Lynn and I went back home with him, and everything was all right for awhile.

I went into labor the night of November 2, 1954, and was in labor all night. The next morning Phil took me to the hospital. He just dropped me off and said the hospital could call him at the pool room when it was over.

At 9:15 a.m. I delivered a boy, seven pounds three ounces and nineteen inches long. I named him Dale.

Phil had made a cute crib for Dale and painted it blue, pink, and white. When we got home with the baby and I put him in the crib, Lynn walked right up to him and stuck her fingers in his eyes, saying "eyes, nose, mouth."

"Honey, don't do that to your little brother," I said, "You might hurt him. He is just a newborn baby just like you were once."

She didn't know what to think of him.

Jed, Phil's brother was married and had four girls. When Dale was born, he would come down to see him, play with him, and hold him for a long time. When he was ready to leave, he'd always ask, "How much would you take for him?"

And I would always answer, "He isn't for sale today. But I'll let you know." And Jed would laugh.

Phil didn't pay as much attention to Dale as he had to Lynn. Even his father noticed that and asked me about it one day. But I didn't know why. He was just never close with Dale.

Phil rented half of a duplex, and we bought some furniture and moved in. It had two bedrooms and a bath.

The young couple in the other half of the duplex had a Labrador tied up in the back yard. When Dale was seven months old, he was sitting in his stroller in the yard while I was hanging up clothes. The dog got loose, and, before I knew it, he was all over Dale, chewing on him.

I grabbed him away from the dog, checked him over, and then took him next door to show them what their dog had done to my baby. They took the dog to the pound. The neighbor was about to have her first baby and didn't want that dog around.

Phil was still drinking. Glenda was staying with us one night. She was asleep on the couch, and I was in my bedroom when I heard her say, "You better leave me alone, or I'm calling Ruthie."

I got up and found Phil sitting on the side of the couch with his hands on her breast. He was so drunk he could hardly walk. I told him to get out, and he left. He didn't come back for days. He lost his job, and we couldn't pay the rent, so we had to move back in with his parents.

By that time I was pregnant again.

Phil found another job in Anderson, Indiana, about an hour's drive away, working the second shift from four p.m. to midnight.

He had been setting out trout lines in Flat Rock River and decided he needed a boat. I helped him build one, and, after he got off work, we would run the lines together. Boy, did we get the catfish.

If Phil wasn't fishing, he was out on the weekends with his friends. He would come home on Friday night, get cleaned up, and take off despite my pleading with him to stay. He would come back on Sunday broke and stinking from drinking booze and not washing. He'd get money from his mother to go to work on Monday.

I went into labor with my third baby, and she was born at 11:15 a.m. on April 27, 1956. She weighed seven pounds even and was twenty inches long. She was a precious little girl, fat as a butterball and curly haired. I named her Kay.

Shortly after we returned to Grandma and Grandpa's house, I discovered that Kay had a bad case of asthma. I was up day and night with her. I put a sheet over her crib and put medicine the doctor gave me in a vaporizer.

After that she got the colic, and for six weeks we all walked the floor with her and rocked her. We were worn out.

Phil never was home to help. He was always out drinking with his Buddies. He was never home on a weekend and then started staying out all night on Wednesdays too.

He would come home and accuse me of running around on him, even though I was with his parents every night taking care of three babies. I would tell him I never did any such thing, but he would pull me out of bed and hit me. I always had a bloody nose and black eyes. Many times his parents would have to pull him off me.

One time his mother told him that he was the one with a guilty conscience and that he had better leave me alone or she would call the police on him.

Not long after that he came in drunk again and started in on me. He nearly pulled the hair out of one side of my head and was beating on me when his parents got up. Dad Willis was trying to get him off of me, and Phil hit his dad and started choking him. His mother cut his nose with an ash tray, leaving a permanent scar. She then went to a neighbor's house and called the police.

When he saw the police, he ran out the back door. A cop shouted to him to stop or he would shoot, and they took him off to jail. The next day his parents went and got him out. I had another black eye and bloody nose. I filed charges against him, and he had to pay a fine. His father wouldn't file charges; he said it was a family matter.

The neighbors asked me why I put up with it. But I loved him and thought he would change. I did threaten to divorce him that time, and he was good to me for awhile.

Phil found us a house with a basement, three bedrooms, and a bath across the street from the house of his oldest brother, Lou, although neither Lou nor his wife ever came over to see us.

Phil set up a bait house in the basement and then bought himself a new blue pickup. He built a cover for the bed of the truck and fitted it with a minnow tank and fishing poles. He made his own sinkers.

He caught his own bait after work. He would go to the golf course and catch worms. On the weekends he would go out in his truck and sell bait along the rivers. And get drunk.

In the basement bait house we had night crawlers, red worms, leaches, minnows, and soft crawfish, along with rods and reels, poles, sinkers, and what have you. The truck was also fully stocked for Phil's weekend river runs.

People came in at all hours of the night looking for bait. Since Phil was usually out catching more bait or drinking with his Buddies, I was the one that had to get up to wait on customers.

I discovered that I had a tumor in my stomach and would need surgery. Phil took me to the hospital and took the kids to Grandma's. At the hospital they injected me with a red dye and started taking x-rays. They had taken only one picture when I got cold chills and passed out.

The doctors told Phil that I was allergic to something in the dye and it almost killed me. I was unconscious for two days. When I came to, Mother, Phil, Norma, and Louise were in my room. Mother was on her knees asking God to save me.

The next day they took a tumor out of me the size of a grapefruit. They had cut me wide open, and I could hardly move for days. I went back to Grandma's to recover. She always took off from work to take care of me. She was good to me, and I loved her very much.

We were there about two months before I got back on my feet and could take care of the kids again. After I went back to my house, Grandma and Grandpa were at the house every night and would take one of the kids back home with them. They always did that wherever we lived.

They would ask the kids, "Do any of you want to go home with Grandma?" At least one always did and sometimes two of them. It seemed like half the time I had only one kid to take care of.

They took the kids fishing. Grandpa always had Dale with him.

I wasn't completely healed up from the surgery when I discovered that I was pregnant again. I had a rough time.

I had to climb up and down the basement stairs to wait on customers, take care of Kay, do my housework and laundry, and fix meals. No matter what time Phil came in, he was always hungry. Lynn helped me watch the other kids and was turning into a little mother herself.

Instead of gaining weight, I began losing it and got skinny as a bone. I was tired all the time. The doctor told me I had to give up the bait business.

Phil hadn't been paying the rent, and we had to move back to his parents' house again. Phil moved his bait house into a garage of a friend of his, but winter was coming, and that ended the bait business for awhile. He was still working the night shift in Anderson, Indiana.

I was eight months pregnant when I caught a bad cold. When Mother came to see me, she insisted I go to the doctor. We called him Dr. Bill, and he was the best doctor in town. After he checked me over, he told the nurse to give me a shot of penicillin. When she did, I went out like a light. I was allergic to the penicillin.

Dr. Bill and the nurse went to work on me, and Mother dropped to her knees to pray. When I came to three hours later, Dr. Bill said he hadn't been sure he could save me. "I did my part and the rest was in God's hands."

Dr. Bill sent me home in an ambulance. When I got inside, the kids didn't know me because I had swollen up so badly. I got better in a week or so.

One night I wanted pumpkin pie, and my mother-in-law was baking it for me. It was about eleven p.m. when my water broke and I went into labor. Grandma went next door to get the neighbor to take me to the hospital.

My pains were coming so fast I couldn't time them. The doctor and I got to the hospital at the same time. My Daddy was in the same hospital and, before I went up to the delivery room, I stopped in to see him and gave him a kiss and a hug.

At 3:02 a.m. January 8, 1958, I had an eight pound three ounce boy, twenty-one inches long. Phil walked in just as he was being born. I named him Allen.

I asked to see the baby, but Dr. Bill said that he was cold and they had put him in a warmer and I could see him in the morning. I was hemorrhaging badly, and the doctor told the nurse to raise my feet as high as she could get them.

When Dr. Bill brought the baby in to me the next morning, his eyes were shiny with tears.

"Dr. Bill," I said, " why do you have tears in your eyes?"

"Ruthie," he said, "the baby was born with two club feet."

Dr. Bill was always emotional if anything happened to his patient or babies.

He showed me Allen's legs, and they were all twisted up. That didn't bother me. I was ready to accept him with open arms just as he was. He was my beautiful son, and all I wanted was to hold him and love him.

Dr. Bill had taped splints on both feet and told me he had already gotten in touch with Dr. Icker, a specialist from Indianapolis, who was on his way down. Dr. Icker put Allen's feet in casts.

The day we were to go home, January 11, 1958, Mother came in to tell me that Daddy had died at seven that morning. He was sixty-two. She told me he had kept asking, "Has Ruthie had her baby yet?" and she would answer, "Yes, she has a fine boy."

I wasn't able to get to his funeral.

I was twenty-one and had four kids by then. I think now about what I put Mother through. She was always there for all her girls.

She had a good life from that point on.

Chapter Nine

Treatment of Allen's club feet was a long process. We used to soak off the casts in Karo syrup and water, and every two weeks we had to go back to Indianapolis.

It seems that Phil was never home when we had to go. I don't remember everyone who helped us get to Indianapolis. His sister and her husband took me often, and I think Norma took us once. Another time, a police officer took us.

After seven months of casts, they put him in two pair of shoes with the toes cut out and a pair he slept in at night with a bar between them. All Allen's shoes looked as if they were for the wrong feet. But by the time he was ten months old he was walking. When he was eleven, they put him in shoes they called straight lines, but he hated them and wouldn't wear them.

The older children helped with the younger ones. When Allen was born, he became Lynn's baby. She was a big help to me by playing with him, and she was the one who taught him how to rock on his bars and then to walk.

Dale loved Kay from the time she was born. Kay was asleep in her baby bed and she woke up and started crying. It was her feeding time, I went to the baby bed and changed her and then went into the kitchen to warm her bottle. I noticed she had stopped crying and when I returned with her bottle I noticed Dale sitting in her baby bed. He had his hands on Kay's head trying to drag her up onto his lap. I put Kay in his lap and helped him hold her bottle while he fed her. Dale said, "see mommy I can help." I told him thanks for helping mommy, I wish I had had a camera that was a beautiful sight to see. Both he and Lynn helped her learn to walk. Dale and Kay looked so cute as they walked together holding hands.

Lynn was always acting like she was a ballerina, or dancer. She would stand up on her tip toes and twirl around and then she would jump up into the air with her legs spread as far apart as she could get them. She would say, "see mommy, watch me, I'm a ballerina dancer." Grandma and I always told her, some day she would make a beautiful ballot dancer. Lynn was so graceful and still is today. But her dream never came true. Dale liked to pick on his daddy's guitar, Allen liked to beat on a tin pan with spoons. .

Dale was always in some kind of mischief when he was a little boy. We lived about a block from the junior high school, and the kids used to park their cars in front of our house. Dale used to get in their cars and blow the horn and turn on their lights. When they got out of school, they would discover their batteries were run down and they couldn't start their cars.

In the winter, Dale would throw snowballs at kids going to school, and some of them would chase him inside the house.

One time Dale and a neighbor boy threw a big rock at a police car and broke the windshield. The neighbor boy's family blamed it all on Dale, but the policeman said he didn't know which boy's rock had hit him. I had to pay for a new windshield.

Dale got more whippings than the other kids. One time when I was trying to give him a spanking, he ran around the table, and I couldn't reach him. So I got the broom and cracked him on the head.

"Mommy, you really hurt my head," he said.

"Well then don't run from me," I told him.

Lynn told me once that she deserved more whippings than she got. The worst whipping with switches that I ever gave her came one day when she was thirteen and sassed me.

Kay got quite a few. She sneaked out of the house one night and went down the street to a little store that stayed open until ten p.m. I followed her to the store, and, when she came out eating a candy bar, I switched her all the way home.

She had been getting too heavy for her size and age, and I had her on a diet at that time. She wasn't supposed to have any candy. I took her to the doctor once, and he told me she had gained two more pounds. I didn't understand how until I was cleaning her room one day and found candy bar wrappers and banana peels under the mattress. However there were times they made me very proud of them. Kay and Lynn both had a beautiful voice. Lynn sang with her cousin Sandy, the preachers' daughter and one of their friends in church. Kay also sang in church with two other girls.

Allen was a good little boy, but he got a few whippings when he acted up at the table. One time he threw a fit in a store when I refused to buy him a toy or something that he wanted. I picked him up and spanked him in front of some people. He looked up at me and said, "Mommy, you embarrassed me."

"You embarrassed me too," I replied.

He told me that Grandma and Grandpa always bought him something. I told him that I wasn't Grandma or Grandpa and when he was with me he wasn't going to get anything he wanted and he had to mind.

Phil was still abusive. We were renting a big two-story house across from a hospital one time when he had been out all night and came in about noon. I was standing at the sink doing dishes when he came up behind me and, without warning, hit me in the back of the head.

As I turned around, he hit me in the mouth, and I fell back and hit my head on the corner of the washing machine. I fell to the floor unconscious.

Phil picked me up and put me on the bed. He got scared and ran across the street to the hospital to get help. He told them that I had slipped and fallen in the kitchen. A doctor and a nurse came to the house, and I was carried to the emergency room on a stretcher.

In the meantime, Dale ran down to a neighbor's house and had them call the police because his daddy was hurting his mommy. Phil took off in his truck before the police got there. Every time I had pressed charges against him for beating on me, he would drive out of town. The police never could catch him.

A nurse went back to the house and got the kids and brought them over to the hospital.

When I woke up, my whole body was shaking and jerking, and I couldn't see clearly. The doctor gave me a shot to settle me down. After awhile I was able to tell the police what Phil had done to me. I was devastated.

The police picked up my mother and told her that she could have Phil arrested on my behalf. She agreed to pressing charges, but the police couldn't find him. She took the kids home with her.

I had a concussion, and my legs were paralyzed for about three days. I had stitches in my upper lip inside and out where a tooth had gone clear through. My face was swollen and black and blue. I spent a week in the hospital.

Kay was about eight at the time. She still remembers the day and says that Phil kept beating on me even after I had fallen to the floor.

There was a write up in the newspaper about it.

Mother and Albert moved into the house with me, and Mother gave me money to start divorce proceedings.

One night I heard a noise and started upstairs to investigate. Phil was standing there, and that scared me to death. I screamed for Mother to call the police. Lloyd came in with a gun and threatened to kill him.

Phil was up on the roof of the house when the police arrived, and he got away. The police told Lloyd that he couldn't legally kill Phil but that I could have because he was in my house and I had a restraining order against him. He wasn't supposed to come anywhere near me. I thought for sure the police would find him and he would be put away for awhile.

I had to watch my back from then on. I went back to work, and Mother took care of the kids for me. Not long after, Mother didn't want to baby sit. She wanted to be free to travel.

After awhile I dropped the divorce and took that fool back. I couldn't afford the house without Mother's help. Mother and Albert got their own place, and we moved back in with Phil's parents. I had no choice. I had been to the welfare agency and to the law. I had no one else to turn to, and I needed a helping hand.

I don't ever remember Phil being home on Easter. The kids and I would go to church. Grandpa Willis would hide the eggs in the yard, one of them gold with a dollar sign on it. Whoever found the gold egg would get five dollars.

Grandma bought all the kids Easter baskets and clothes. One year she dressed the girls alike with pretty pink dresses, black patent leather shoes, and ribbons in their hair. The boys were all dressed in their little suits and new shoes.

They were beautiful kids. The neighbors used to tell me that if I didn't stop giving them so many baths I was going to wash their skin off.

I used to take them to the park and play with them. I taught them how to skate and ride their bikes.

Dale would go fishing with Grandpa and would always come home with some fish. When I asked Grandpa if Dale caught the fish himself, he would say, "Yes, with a little help once in awhile."

Dale would take the fish over to Virginia, one of our neighbors who loved catfish, and she would pay him for them.   One time when Dale was about four, I told Grandpa that I was going to take the kids and go visit my friend Beth--she had three kids at the time--so that I might not be home when he brought him back from fishing. Grandpa was running late when he got back, and he was in a hurry to pick Grandma up from work. So he just let Dale out and drove away.

While he was alone in the house, Dale began playing with some matches he found and set the kitchen curtains on fire. He ran out of the house and told the neighbors the house was on fire. They called the fire department.

When I got home, the firemen were still there, and Dale was crying. He told the firemen that he would get a whipping when Mommy got home.

When Grandma and Grandpa arrived, Grandpa said only that he had forgotten that I wouldn't be home.

When he was about five, Dale won a five-dollar savings account and a trophy for catching the biggest fish in a parks and recreation department fishing tournament. He got his picture in the paper.

One time Grandpa brought him home with a fish hook in his thumb, and I had to take him to the emergency room to get it taken out. He never cried.

That wasn't the only time I had to take him to the emergency room. Another time he cut his foot in the park, and I had to take him to the hospital for stitches. The doctors got to know Dale well.

Once when I was giving the boys a bath, Dale ran out of the bathroom soaking wet. He liked to tease me. He ran into the living room, and, when Grandpa saw him, he took off his belt and whipped him. By the time I got to the living room, Dale had big welts on him.

I jumped on Grandpa's back and began beating on him. I told him never to touch one of my kids again, and he never did.

Dale got his own paper route when he was eleven and used some of his earnings to buy a bicycle and a .410 shotgun he used for hunting squirrels and rabbits.

In the winter Dale would shovel snow for elderly people or go to the store for them, and sometimes they would give him some money.

I always knew where the kids were. Kay would be at her girlfriend's house, and the other three would be sitting on the porch entertaining some of the elderly couples.

Chapter Ten

One time when I was so sick I had been hospitalized, I took a turn for the worse. The hospital called and asked for Phil, but he wasn't anywhere to be found. Dad Willis was the only one home, and he was the one who was sitting by my bedside when I woke up. "I'm glad to see you awake," he said. " I'll get Mom".

I called my in-laws Mom and Dad because they treated me like a daughter. When Dad and Mom Willis came back, they had my children with them. The kids stood outside on the lawn waving at me and throwing me kisses. I felt very lucky to have a bed by the window. I can still see my babies waving at me.

Many times it was Dad Willis who took me to the doctor when Phil wasn't home. After he retired, he helped me out by watching the kids when I was washing clothes or cleaning house.

It was 1959, and I was 22 and pregnant for the fifth time.

I got pregnant again when Allen was still a baby. When I told Phil, he got mad, he didn't want another baby.

Soon after that he lost his job in Anderson, and we were without insurance. He went to work at a junk yard taking parts off old and wrecked cars. He was gone more and more, often for three or four days and nights at a time. Then he got a job driving a semi tractor and trailer for a friend of his to and from Florida and would sometimes be gone for a week or a two at a time. He would call his mother for money to get home on.

He would never sit at the table and eat with us. I had to carry his food into the living room where he sat in his chair watching TV. I had to wait on him hand and foot.

When he wanted sex, he would begin by slapping me around or beating me. Then we had sex, and he acted as if that made up for the beating.

The strong love I'd had for him in the beginning died slowly, and I began to hate him.

When I was five and a half months pregnant Phil came in about two o'clock in the morning. I heard him stumbling up to the door, I got right up to let him in. He came in drunk and in a rage, as soon as I opened the door he hit me in the stomach, I fell and hit the corner of the kitchen table. I felt the baby move. He started pushing me towards the bedroom, as soon as we got in bed he wanted sex. He ripped my under pants off and my gown and bent my legs over my head, he had my arms pinned down with his hands. I was doubled up tight and he was so rough on me that I kept saying to him you are going to hurt the baby and you are hurting me. He forced himself inside me, It felt like he was tearing me apart , from the weight of his body it felt like he was breaking my back. I felt my baby moving, I knew the baby was in pain. Phil murdered our baby. The baby got in a hard knot like a ball and I was in severe pain. I managed to get my right leg down far enough and kicked him off of me and on to the floor. I was horrified.

Mom Willis got up and wanted to know what was going on. I got out of bed and started rubbing my stomach to get the baby to move, I was terrified. After awhile I felt a slight movement like the baby relaxed, the baby never moved again. It was no-longer the pain of the flesh but the pain of my spirit had just been crushed out of me. I wanted to die from the emotional and eternal pain I knew I would feel for the rest of my life if what I had suspected had really happened to me that dreadful night.

Phil could never have hurt me more than he had that night. You can blame booze, you can blame any excuse that could ever be described and you would never convince me that there is a greater pain than the murder of a baby in a mother's womb. I began to call out to God for the only help I knew could foster and care for me through this more than a horrifying experience. What had I done, dear God to deserve this pain in my life?

I cried out for God to forgive me for not caring for one of His own, one of my own.

I told his mother Phil just killed our baby, I knew what had happened to my baby and me. Mom Willis sat up with me the rest of the night trying to comfort me. At eight AM when the doctors office opened I called for an appointment, I told the nurse it was very important that I get right in to see doctor Bill, the nurse told me to come in at ten AM. I told Dr. Bill what Phil had done to me, I told him my baby is dead He checked for a heart beat but couldn't hear anything. I told him the baby had not moved since the incident. he gave me another appointment to come back in a week for sure, that went on for about four weeks and still no movement or heart beat from the baby. The last time I went to see Dr. Bill I was very sick and all swelled up and had a 103 fever. My hands and feet were so big I could hardly walk into his office. Phil went with me to the doctor this time. It was on Thursday when doctor Bill took one look at me and told his nurse to take a blood sample and take it right over to the hospital for a blood test and he wanted a report right away, and he confirmed that the baby was dead. Dr. Bill gave Phil a real good talking to. He said to Phil what kind of a man are you to do such a thing to your wife and child. Dr. Bill said we had to sign some papers for a procedure to be performed. He told Phil to sign the papers and get out of his office and told him he never wanted to see him again. Phil signed the papers and walked out of the office to his car. I signed the papers and so did Dr. Bill and his nurse. Dr. Bill gave me a prescription for antibiotics, I was to take them four times a day with butter milk, about 4 PM that same day Dr. Bill called me and told me I had blood poison. Dr. Bill told me he would perform a procedure and explained to me that he would go up inside me and clip me in a couple of places to put me in labor. Since I had blood poison they could not do a caesarean because as soon as they opened me up I would have died. Dr. Bill told me to come back Friday at 1:00 PM for the procedure. I called Glenda and she took me, after the procedure was done on the way home Glenda said "Sis did that hurt very much"?, I said "yes but something had to be done or else I was going to die". Later that day Phil came home, I told him what had happened and that I could go into labor any time and that Dr. Bill said to tell you not to leave me for any reason. He said, "nobody tells me what to do" he answered and took off. I begged him not to leave me and asked him, "don't you care what the doctor said", he left anyway. Phil didn't come home until the next morning when my sister Glenda was taking me to the hospital. He said to me, "where do you think you are going?", he was so drunk he told me to get back in the house, I just kept on walking, best I could to Glenda's car. When she left me at the hospital she had to be at work at 6 AM and she was late.

Back in 1959 there were sixteen steps up to the front door of the hospital. I started up the steps and I heard a mans voice say lady you look like you need some help, I said "yes sir, I do", he put his arms around my waist and held on to my hand all the way up into the hospital admission office. He looked to be about 35 or 40 years old. I said ,"thank you so much because I didn't know how I was going to get up all those steps", I could hardly walk. When Glenda got to work she called Norma who brought our Mother to the hospital to be with me. I went into labor about 6 AM Saturday, February 7th, 1959. They kept me in the labor room because I had blood poisoning and they didn't want to infect the delivery room. I noticed my labor pains were coming up the sides of my stomach and down my back. Every time I had a pain the baby would get under my ribs and cut off my breath, Dr. Bill said to let him know the next time the pain started, when I told him he told the nurse to lay across my stomach. When she did it was like I floated out of my body. I was in bed sitting up with a sheet over me floating through this real bright light which was all around me. I could see myself lying in a bed, I could see my mother on her knee's beside the bed, I was waving good bye to mother and telling her I was at peace and happy. At last, when I returned to my body I already had the baby. God saved me from going through the pain of delivery of my still born son. At 10 AM Saturday morning I had a perfect and most beautiful little boy. He weighed one pound and thirteen ounces. The doctor said he had been bigger but had shrunk. I told Dr. Bill and Mother about my experience, I said I died didn't I, Dr. Bill said we almost lost you but it wasn't your time to go and God answered your mothers prayers. I asked Dr. Bill what killed my baby, he said I'm not sure but he could have a broken neck or suffocated depending on what position he was in at the time of the incident. I begged Dr. Bill to let me see the baby, he didn't want to but I insisted and finally he brought my son in a dish pan and I got to see my tiny beautiful son, I named him Bryan Wayne. He smelled rotten and was blue and gray color. He had blond hair on his little head, His eyes were sunk back in his little head. He had thin fingernails on his fingers and on his toes. I couldn't touch him or hold him because he was decaying. Mother also got to see Bryan and we both agreed he looked like his brother Allen. Re-living the death of my son sends sharp pains through my heart, I can't explain the pain and I can't hold back my tears. My mother was on her knees again praying for me. This has been very painful for me to write, it hurts worse than anything Phil had ever done to me. When the nurse wheeled me back into the ward with other new mothers she told them this one had bad luck, she said it as if what she had seen me go through didn't bother her a bit. But it sure hurt me and when they brought the other babies in to be fed I just laid in my bed crying over the loss of my son. It was cruel of the nurse to have put me in with the other new mothers. I should have had a room to myself. I know Bryan is in heaven and I will get to see him again some day.

After I got settled into my room Dr. Bill came in and asked me where Phil was, I told him he was home drunk. Dr. Bill called the house and asked for Phil but his mother said she couldn't get him awake. I told Dr. Bill to call Murphy's funeral home to come and get the baby. When Mr. Murphy came to pick up my baby he came in to talk to me about the funeral arrangements, he said the only thing they could do was to pack my baby in cotton and they would put him in a little blue casket. He asked me what I had named him, I said Bryan Wayne, he told me he would be buried on Monday at 10:30 AM. I told Mr. Murphy I wanted a grave site service. Phil never did come see me in the hospital, he got the grave site and that was it. Mom Willis told me later that Mr. Murphy came by the house on Monday to get Phil to attend the grave side services , Phil refused to go and Mr. Murphy told him he was going to go and if he refused to go he would call the police to force him to go.

Dr. Bill came in on Wednesday morning to tell me I was being released to go home. He handed me two prescriptions, one was for the antibiotics 4 times a day with a glass of butter milk, the other prescription was for a new birth control that was 99% sure I wouldn't get pregnant again. Dr. Bill told me I would be on antibiotics for a long time until all the blood poison was out of my system. Dr. Bill wished me good luck. I called my brother-in-law Bob at the police station that was only a block or two from the hospital, I told him I had been released and asked him if he could come and take me home, he said I'll be right there. I sat in the back seat on the way home, it seemed to take a long time. I had all these mixed feelings stirring up inside me, I was sad, lonely and empty inside. I was going home without my precious son and what was I going to tell my children that loved to put their little hands on my stomach when the baby was moving. I was still all swelled up with the blood poisoning . Bob helped me out of the car and into the house. Mom Willis opened the door for us, I walked in and sat down in our big chair in the living room.

Lynn was in school, Dale, Kay, and Allen came up to me with big smiles on their little faces. Allen was just a little toddler, Dale was four, and Kay was three. I gave them big hugs and kisses and Allen crawled up onto my lap, Kay sat on the other side of me in the chair. They were so happy to see me, Dale said mommy where is the baby?, I told him he had another little baby brother and Jesus wanted him to live in heaven with him. Dale said mommy what did Jesus name him?, I said Bryan Wayne. Mom and Dad Willis were sitting on the couch and didn't say a word. The kids started playing and I started crying. Dale said mommy why are you crying, I told him I was so happy to be back home. But that wasn't the real reason, I was crying over the night the baby died inside me. Mom said Ruth do you want a cup of coffee and a piece of pie?, I said yes but I'll go to the table. Mom sat at the table with me she said I'm so sorry for what happened to you and the baby. I told her I understand she had no words to comfort me. Not another word was spoken about the baby. Phil went on with his life as usual and I felt very alone with my sorrow, I had four children who needed me and each day they helped me to get better, I didn't have time to think so much. For weeks I went through pure hell, just devastated, I couldn't eat or sleep, I was very restless.

I learned later that Phil was in a tavern dancing. My sister Louise was there. She hadn't heard about the baby yet, and when Phil asked her to dance with him, she did. He told her then that I had lost the baby. "What are you doing here, then? Why aren't you with Ruth?" she asked him. She walked away from him on the dance floor and left.

Phil couldn't have cared less about me. All he wanted to do was drink and have fun. When I went home, he acted as if nothing had happened, and I wouldn't talk to him. All my feelings for him had gone. They had died with the baby.

When I felt up to it, I went to visit Bryan's grave. I had my silent talk with him and prayed. I know Bryan is in heaven, and I will see him again some day. Thank God he didn't have to go through the pain and suffering his brothers and sisters went through.

Every time I go home for a visit, I go to the graveyard and put flowers on his little grave. He lives in my heart and is with me wherever I go.

I wanted to get a divorce right away, but I didn't have the money nor any place to go with four kids. Mother's place wasn't big enough, and none of my sisters could take us all in. So I was stuck for awhile.

I had myself sterilized so I couldn't have any more children.

Phil came home one day and told me we were going to move to the country. He had rented a two-story farmhouse with a barn. He bought two four-day-old calves that we had to feed by hand. We also got a dog.

The kids and I loved the farmhouse. Phil was being good at the time. He would make his runs to Florida with the semi and would be gone for a week. In 1960 I went to work in a factory, I worked the 3 to 11 shift.

My brother Lloyd and his wife would baby sit for me. That worked really well for awhile. One day a taxi pulled up in front of the house, and a girl with a three-month-old baby girl got out and came to the door looking for Phil.

She said her name was Jackie and Phil was the baby's father.

Phil had brought her back from Florida and had been living with her off and on in an apartment in Fairland. That explained all the time he had been spending away from home and the fact that he never had any money.

She told me Phil hadn't paid the rent, and she had been kicked out of the apartment. I told her Phil was away with the truck and I didn't know where he was. She left with the baby. A few day's later she showed up at his mother's house.

Phil came home about 2:30 one morning, and I told him his girlfriend was at his mother's. He left and didn't come back for two weeks. I guess he took Jackie back to Florida.

Phil came in one morning and wanted me to have oral sex with him. I refused and he started banging my head into the wall. Then he grabbed my groin and started pulling out my pubic hair. He pulled so hard until I couldn't stand it any more and gave in and he had sex with me. He said didn't that feel better. I was in so much pain I just cried it hurt so bad. He said just look at you, you are nothing but a cry baby. I said I wonder why, is that what you think about me? I mean nothing to you. He just grinned at me. I was sore and had a hard time walking for awhile. I had a sore head and a swelled up face with bruises. My dog jumped up on the bed and bit him. He got out of bed and kicked the dog across the room, then told me to fix him some peanut butter sandwiches because he was hungry.

He went to the bathroom and I began fixing the sandwiches. We had rats in the barn and mice in the house and I had bought some rat poison. I took it out and put some of it on one of the sandwiches.

Phil came out and ate the first sandwich and started on the one with the rat poison. He told me it didn't taste right and I told him the peanut butter was probably old. He ate about half of it and threw the rest away. I started laughing and when he asked why, I told him. He took out of the house like lightning and rushed to the hospital to get his stomach pumped. He didn't come back for a long time.

I had enough of his beatings and really felt like killing him. He could have had me arrested but he didn't. He came back one night, got his calves and all his clothes and left

The weather turned cold, and I had to order some oil. I got $100 worth and went to work. I woke up about four the next morning, and the house was cold. The furnace was off, and, when I checked the oil barrels, they were empty. I took the kids and went to my mother's.

Albert told me the next day that Lloyd and another man had taken my oil and sold it. Winter was bitter cold, and I knew I couldn't make it on my own. Phil wasn't giving me any money for support. I hung in for a while longer. Then one morning I discovered that my car was gone. I finally found it wrecked in a ditch across the road.

Phil had taken it during the night, wrecked it, and left.

That day he came back and started in on me. I called out to Louise to come.

He sneered at me, "Do you think your big sister can protect you?"

Louise came flying in with a baseball bat and sat down. When he started pushing me around, she jumped right in his face.

"You lay one hand on her, and you are going to get this baseball bat right up against your head."

The sparks were flying out of her green eyes.

I had called the police, and they came and took him to jail.

Since I no longer had a car, I couldn't get to work. We had to move back in with Phil's parents. After a couple of days, his parents got him out of jail because, they said, he had to work. As if that made any difference.

Phil's mother retired, and I had it a little easier. She took care of the kids for me while I worked from three to eleven p.m. in the factory. Things went all right for a while longer. Then one day while doing the laundry I found some black and yellow pills in Phil's shirt pocket.

I showed them to the doctor next time I saw him, and he said they were a stimulant that truck drivers used to stay awake. They called them yellow jackets. Dr. Bill said that they should never be mixed with alcohol, and they were probably part of what made Phil so crazy.

Dr. Bill went on vacation for a couple of months and told me that if I needed a doctor while he was gone to go to Dr. Dunn, a new doctor in town. Dr. Dunn became my new doctor.

Phil didn't have any health insurance, but I had a good policy where I worked, and I covered all of us. It was a good thing I did. The phone rang many times when one of the kids got hurt and had to be taken to the emergency room. And I was in and out of the hospital myself. I had surgery three times.

One night Phil came to pick me up from work. He was drunk. Instead of taking me home, he drove out into the country to an old viaduct bridge over a river. He began beating me. He had been in a fight with my brother Lloyd in a tavern, and Lloyd had given him a big knot on his head. He was afraid of Lloyd.

When he started beating me, he told me he was going to show me what he thought of Lloyd.

He smashed my nose and broke my mouth wide open. I was bleeding so badly that my white blouse was covered with blood.

64

I was in and out of consciousness each time Phil hit me. When I came to, I was choking on blood running down my throat from my mouth and gasping for my breath. Phil was slapping my face and shaking me. I was so dazed and couldn't see clearly. I finally came to my senses. As I face reality today I could have died that night. I tried to get out of the car to run to a house for help, but he grabbed me and told me if I got out, he'd take me to the river and drown me. I knew he really would, so I stayed in the car.

He had sex with me while I was covered with blood and begging him to leave me alone.

It was dawn when he took me home. His mother saw us coming and opened the door. She looked at me with tears in her eyes. When I went to the bathroom and took off my clothes, she came in and put them in cold water to soak.

"Phil did this to you?" she asked.

I nodded my head yes and went to bed. Later I tried to get up to go to the bathroom, but I couldn't lift my head off the bed. I called Grandma to help me up. When I looked in the mirror, I saw I had two black eyes, and my mouth and nose were so swollen I couldn't even recognize myself.

The kids got up and asked me if it hurt much. Phil told them I hit a tree.

"No, Daddy," Dale said. "You did this to Mommy, and when I grow up I'm going to beat you up."

Phil just thought that was funny. He asked me, "Do you like the new face I gave you?"

He had no feelings for me. He would never even say he was sorry.

His mother took good care of me. She made me chicken soup to sip through a straw and made milkshakes for me.

I was in bed for more than a week, and Phil didn't leave the house. He knew that if I could get out, I would go to the police. He finally left one morning, and I walked to Norma's house. My face was still swollen, and the bruises were green and purple. Norma took one look at me and cried her heart out.

I asked her to take me to work so I could get my paycheck. When they saw the way I looked, my boss said somebody ought to kill that so and so. I went back to work in about two weeks.

One day I was sitting on a stool at a machine and passed out and fell to the floor. When I woke up, I was in the hospital.

All I could do was cry, day and night. I didn't know what I could do to get away from Phil and take my kids with me. I couldn't bring myself to tell the doctor just how bad things were.

"Ruth," he said finally, "you're having a nervous breakdown, and I can't treat you if you don't tell me why."

But I wouldn't tell anyone.

One morning the doctor came in and said they were taking me to another room for a test. They put a needle in my arm, and I didn't know anything until I was back in my room. I wasn't crying anymore, and there was a police guard at my door.

Poor little Dale came up to see me. He had told the nurse he was fourteen--he was about nine--and she pretended that she believed him and let him come up. She told me later that boy really wanted to see his mommy and she wasn't going to stop him.

Dale wanted to know why there was a policeman at my door. "Did you do something bad?"

I told him no, that the policeman was there to protect me.

The doctor came in later in the day and told me he had given me truth serum to find out what was going on. He told me that if I didn't divorce that animal, I either liked what he was doing to me or I was crazy.

He told me the truth serum test could be used in court. Otherwise, it would be kept as a private record in the hospital and even I couldn't get to see it. I didn't need to; I lived it.

Phil tried to come and see me, but the guard stopped him, and he left. He then called Dr. Dunn at three one Sunday morning. Phil was drunk, and he accused Dr. Dunn of being my lover and keeping me under protection for his own use. He threatened the doctor.

Dr. Dunn told me about it the next day and said that if Phil called him again, he would have him arrested. I told him he should do just that, and I said I was sorry.

Dr. Dunn said he would go to court with me and bring the records from the hospital if I needed him for my divorce. I thought that was very kind of him.

When I was dismissed, my brother-in-law Bob came to take me home.

"Ruth," he said, "I don't know how much more you can take from Phil."

"I'm going to have to do something," I told him, "or I won't live to see my kids grow up."

Chapter Eleven

I did talk to the welfare people, and a woman told me that if I would let them place my kids in foster homes, I could get rid of Phil. I told her I would die before I would give up my kids.

Phil had no love or passion or feeling for anyone and always took what he wanted from others. He didn't see anything wrong with how he spent his money or lived his life.

He was at his worst after he had gotten into it at a tavern with someone he couldn't hurt. He would come home angry and take it out on the kids or me. He always had to have the upper hand and was always hurting those that couldn't hurt him back. He was a full-blown coward.

He once beat my brother Gene with a pair of knucks because Gene knew he had been going with one of our cousins and was going to tell me. Phil was a big man with very large hands, and you never knew which one he was going to hit you with.

Glenda came to see me once after Phil had beaten me. I had a terrible black eye and was all bruised up. When she saw me, she started crying and said, "Sis, Phil is going to kill you if you don't get away from him."

While that was going on, life continued more normally in other areas. Mom Willis taught me how to cook, for example.

Once when she was trying to teach me how to make gravy, I made it so thick you could cut it with a knife. We had a big laugh out of that. But she didn't give up on me.

Eventually I learned how to make gravy. In fact, I turned out to be a good cook. I usually did the cooking while she did the baking. She could bake the best pies and cakes I have ever eaten. I wanted to learn to bake like she did, but she just used a pinch of this and a pinch of that, and I could never get the hang of it. I never could make a crust as good as hers.

One time Dad Willis asked my father to build a fence around our backyard. It took him about a week, and I fixed him a good dinner every day. One time it was fried chicken with all the trimmings, and Daddy said, "Ruthie, this is the best fried chicken I have ever eaten."

He told me I had turned out to be a good cook, and that made me very proud.

He also liked Mom Willis' pies, particularly her cherry pie.

Norma and Junior also loved her cherry pies. I liked them all, but chocolate was my favorite.

While Mom and I did everything together in the kitchen, Dad Willis watched and played with the kids.

If Phil was home, all he would do is sit in his chair and yell and scream at me and the kids, or order me around as if he were a king on his throne. All he was good for was making babies, not helping me raise them. He told me that I had the kids and they belonged to me, as if he had nothing to do with it. He never did anything with the kids and never had any time for them.

He never had any time for me either unless he wanted sex. I guess he thought that was all there was to marriage.

I was always finding pills in his pants pockets and lipstick on his shirt collar. After being gone for three or four days, he would come in smelling like a brewery.

Wages weren't very good back then, and I wasn't making enough to support me and our four kids. Phil never gave me any money. In fact, sometimes he took money from me.

I got paid on Thursdays, and one Thursday evening Phil came over to where I worked and demanded my paycheck. I knew he would cause a scene if I didn't give it to him and that might get me fired, so I signed my check and gave it to him. He left, and I didn't see him again until he had spent all of my paycheck having a good time.

I often wondered where Phil got the money he did have because he didn't work half the time. His mother and father bought all the clothes for me and the kids and made sure the kids had a good Christmas and Easter.

One time Phil did buy me a new dress and told me I looked cute in it with my black eye. Another time he came home with a set of diamond rings, each set with five diamonds in the shape of a heart. Later I sold them to Gene when he married his second wife.

The only times that Phil helped out were when we were living by ourselves. But then he wouldn't pay all the rent and the utilities, and we would get behind. The electric or gas company was always coming out to shut off our lights or gas, and we would end up back with his parents.

One time, for example, I was cooking the kids' lunch when a man from the gas company came out to shut the gas off. I asked him if he could wait until I was finished cooking lunch, and he said he would come back at one p.m. When he came back at one p.m., the electric man was right behind him, and they shut off both the lights and gas. I had to call Phil's parents to come and get us.

The welfare people wouldn't help at that time because I was married. And, even if I had gotten a divorce, they wouldn't have helped if I had a job.

We lived on and off with Phil's parents for thirteen years.

I never understood why they always took us back in and why they didn't insist Phil stay in his own place and raise his own family. I thought that the reason people got married was to make a home of their own.

I asked Dad Willis one time if Phil had ever had any discipline, if he had ever been spanked. Dad said that Mom Willis would never let him and Phil had always been spoiled rotten. Phil could always get around his mother.

I know she loved me and the kids and was trying to make things easier for us. But by then she was as scared of Phil as I was.

Mom and Dad Willis and the kids and I went on many picnics together, often with Norma and Junior and their five kids. We would go to Flat Rock River to swim and fish. Phil was very seldom around to go with us. Once when he did come along, he brought his boat and didn't even take his own kids for a ride in it. He took my two nieces down the river and didn't come back for a long time. That made me mad.

One Saturday afternoon Phil came home drunk and started in on me. He pulled off all my clothes and pushed me out the front door naked in front of the neighbors who were sitting on their front porch. I ran around to the back of the house and got an old potato sack out of the garage and went to another neighbor's house. She gave me a house coat to put on. I was terribly embarrassed and ashamed to show my face.

I told them I was sorry that they had to see me like that, but they told me they knew what was going on and knew it wasn't my fault. They told me I should take the kids and run away.

They called the police, but as usual Phil got away. Sometimes I think Phil had something going with the police department because they never did much to protect me.

Phil spent a lot of time in Florida and very little with his own family. He surely did miss out on being with four beautiful kids. Even when he was with us, he paid little attention to us. He took us to the zoo in Ohio, for example, but didn't go on a single ride with his kids. He went on all the rides with my nieces.

Another time he was on a picnic with us and was out in the water playing with my nieces. Kay, who had broken her arm and had a cast on it, followed him out into deep water. She nearly drowned, but he didn't even notice until I screamed at him from the river bank to get the baby.

One of the times we had a place of our own was when Phil was buying a two-bedroom, one-bath yellow house that needed a lot of work. He put in a new shower and new floors, redid the kitchen and painted the house inside and out. It was really nice when it was finished and we moved in.

One morning shortly after that, however, Phil got mad about something at breakfast. He picked up his food and threw it to the ceiling, then turned the table over. The kids were afraid to move or make a sound. We were all scared to death.

I told Phil to get out, and he went next door to our neighbors and stayed with them. They were just as bad as he was. The neighbor woman's sister was staying with her, and Phil was going with her, although I didn't know it at the time.

A few days later I took the kids to visit a friend. When we returned, Phil was in the house with his girlfriend and wouldn't let us in. Mother and I went for the police. When we returned, there was trash and dog excrement all over the porch. Mother and one of the police officers stepped in it and got it all over their shoes. The policeman was furious, and, when Phil opened the door, the policeman told him he had twenty-four hours to get out.

The next day the policeman and I went back to the house. The trash was gone from the porch, but, when we opened the door, we found it strung everywhere in the house. Phil had torn the shower apart, and parts of it were lying in every room.

The kitchen was a total mess. There was food from the refrigerator on the walls and all over the stove. The refrigerator, stove, washer, and dryer had all been unplugged and shoved into the middle of the floor.

"What kind of a nut would do this to his family?" the policeman asked me as he helped me put the stove and refrigerator back in place. "Lady," he said, "you'd better divorce this guy. He's crazy!"

I always got plenty of advice, but no one ever volunteered to take me and the four kids.

My sister-in-law Betty helped me clean up, and my brother Gene put the shower back together and hooked up the washer and dryer.

The next day I filed for divorce for the second time.

After we had been separated for awhile, Phil joined a church. About a month after that, Phil and the preacher came by the house. The preacher said that Phil had been saved and wanted to get his wife and family back together. Phil got on his knees and begged me to forgive him and take him back.

I thought he was a new man. I dropped my divorce, and he moved back in. We all went to church together for awhile. But one Sunday, Phil said he didn't feel well enough to go to church, and he never went again. He treated us pretty well for awhile, but then he went back to being his old self. I told Phil that was very low of him to use a preacher and the church to get his own way.

He called from a tavern one time and told me he would be home in a few minutes. So when his friend Jim stopped by a little later, I told him to come in and have a seat because Phil would be right home. A half hour later, Phil still hadn't got home, and Jim left.

Phil was gone all night. When he got in the next day, he told me he had seen Jim and learned he had been there. He accused me of going to bed with Jim and gave me such a terrible beating I couldn't go to work for a week. He then left because he knew I would call the police.

One side of my face was all swollen and black and blue. Later I had to go to the doctor and have a blood clot removed from my ear. The doctor told me to come back if I had any more hearing problems.

When the police came, Dale told them that Daddy had hurt Mommy badly, and all the kids were scared. The police tried to calm us all down. I knew that was as far as it would go. If they had wanted him badly enough, they would have found him.

Sometimes he was there when they arrived, and all they did was give him a talking to. When they left, he would just laugh and say he could get by with anything. He always did.

One night I heard voices in the living room and went in. Phil, drunk as usual, was covering up a woman lying on the couch.

"What do you think you're doing bringing a woman home with you?" I asked him.

"She didn't have anywhere to stay," he said, laughing. "What are you going to do about it?"

"Come morning, neither of you will have a place to stay," I said, "because I'll get a divorce and put a restraining order on you."

He just laughed again, and the two of them left.

One Friday night after he had been gone a week or so, one of my sisters-in-law took me to a tavern where Phil was dancing with one of my cousins. My sister-in-law told me that Phil had been living with her.

"You make a good pair," I told them and walked out.

One night in 1963, when Phil happened to be home and sober, I got a call about three in the morning from a neighbor of his mother telling me that Phil's father had just died.

Phil went over to his mother's house. When he came back, he had Lynn with him. She had been staying with them. She was crying and told me, "Mommy, I saw Grandpa die." I comforted her until she went to sleep.

One night some time after that, Phil came home and dragged me out of bed by my hair. I landed on my hip and bruised it so badly I could hardly walk the next day. My head was so sore that I couldn't comb my hair for days.

Phil had told me that the way to keep a woman home and in her place was to keep her barefoot and pregnant and to beat her once in awhile to show her who's boss.

I told him that he must really hate me to treat me the way he did. He told me he didn't hate me, he loved me. I told him that if that was his idea of love, I didn't want any more of it.

One day when Phil was sober, I tried to have a serious talk with him. I asked him what I did to deserve what he did to me. He admitted that I didn't deserve it.

"When I get to drinking, it makes me crazy."

"If you know that," I said, "why don't you at least stay away from home until you're sober?"

I asked him to stop drinking and get some help before it was too late. But everything I told him went in one ear and out the other.

Finally I warned him, "One night when you come sneaking into the bedroom, you aren't going to know what hit you."

"Are you threatening me?" he asked.

"Take it any way you want," I said. "I'm tired of your abuse."

He beat me for all kinds of reasons. Many times it was because I wouldn't leave the children alone in the house and go out drinking with him and his friends. Phil would say that we would be back before the children got up, but I wouldn't leave them alone.

I thought that sometime it was going to become a matter of him or me. I considered buying a handgun but could never scrape up the money. At any rate, I decided that he wasn't worth spending my life in prison for. But many times I had murder in my heart, and it was only by the grace of God that I never went through with it.

One night I was sound asleep and suddenly felt as if I were drowning. I sputtered awake and found Phil standing beside the bed with a pan in his hand. He had just poured cold water in my face, and I was soaking wet.

"Did I scare you?" he asked, laughing.

"I thought I was dreaming, but I should know better by now," I said. "What is your problem?"

I hated having sex with him. But I knew if I didn't he would only hurt me worse.

He told me he didn't have a problem and then had sex with me. Later I asked him why he did things like pouring cold water on me.

"I was just having fun," he said. He told me that since my side of the bed was wet, I could sleep on the couch. I changed my nightgown and lay down on the couch, but I didn't get any sleep because I didn't know what he would do next.

The final straw came the morning he came in and told me to fix him a bacon sandwich. I got up and fried the bacon the way he liked it. But when I handed it to him, he said, "This isn't done enough."

So I fried it until it was nearly burnt and gave it to him again. He got mad.

"Since you don't know how to fry bacon," he said, "I'll have to show you."

He got some raw bacon from the refrigerator and tried to make me eat it. I bit his finger. He rubbed the bacon all over my face and hair and then had sex with me.

The sight of Phil terrified me, and I knew I couldn't take any more. I knew that was the end.

Chapter Twelve

After he left in the morning I called a taxi and went to Mother's and asked her to go to a lawyer with me right then. I went to the lawyer's office with bits of bacon still in my hair and filed for divorce. It was the third time, and the last. I had dropped the previous suits, but this time I went through with it.

My poor kids stayed with Grandma, and I lived with my mother and brother Albert while I waited for the divorce to go through.

Phil met my brother Gene uptown, and they got into it. Gene got the worst of it. Phil broke his false teeth and blackened both his eyes. In fact, Gene looked just about like I looked after Phil beat me up. I cried when I saw him.

My mother went into a rage. Lloyd, Louise, and Gene's wife went looking for Phil with ball bats and chains intending to give him a whipping he would never forget. But they didn't find him.

I bought a car from Norma and Junior, a very nice 1959 Studebaker Lark.

By the time we got to court, my lawyer had become a judge, and I had a new lawyer. Phil had found himself another woman, and she was two months pregnant.

When Phil got on the witness stand, he told about the time I had fed him rat poison and tried to kill him. The judge told him it was a shame that I hadn't.

His mother testified that I never came to see the kids. Phil and his new woman were living with her, and I went to see the kids only when he wasn't there.

She also testified that I didn't even help with the food. She was lying. I not only had the grocery store receipts, but the man from the grocery store as a witness. He told the judge that I paid the bills.

Phil's mother started crying and said that she lied because Phil told her to and she was afraid of him.

After thirteen years of pure hell, I received my divorce in October 1964. I was twenty-seven and finally free from the maniac.

I have never been able to understand how the gentle person I had fallen in love with had become such an animal. If I had been a bad woman and run around on him, or a bad mother, then maybe I would have deserved what he did to me. But I was a good wife and mother.

Phil remarried twice after we were divorced. Neither wife lived with him very long. They both divorced him. He stayed single for a long time and then just lived with another woman, in and out of his mother's house.

But he hadn't changed. He hit his mother one time and tore her house up. She had him arrested, and he went to prison for six months.

After a few years, Phil married a younger girl and had three more children.

For awhile after the divorce he still harassed me. One time he sideswiped my car when it was parked in front of my mother's house, knocking off the mirror and leaving a big scratch down the side.

Chapter Thirteen

Eventually I met Brad, a handsome man with beautiful red hair, from Rushville, Indiana. We started dating. He was divorced and had three children. I told him about my four children living with their Grandma Willis.

He took me to meet his parents, his sister, and his brother and family. His mother was a nurse who worked at the hospital. They were all very nice and kind to me.

After a couple of months, everyone in my family had become very fond of him. He treated me and my children very well. I thought he was an ideal man and didn't hesitate when he asked me to marry him on December 10, 1964.

Gene and his wife stood up with us, and we were married. Shortly after, he asked me to take my kids and move to California with him. Phil was causing us a lot of trouble, and I thought that was a good idea. Brad sold his car to my brother Gene, and I quit my job.

It was a sad day for Grandma Willis when she had to say goodbye to the kids and knew they would be living so far away. By the time we got to Albuquerque, New Mexico, Dale had gotten so upset at leaving Grandma that he threw a fit, trying to get out the back door of the car.

We finally took him to a bus station, and I asked if the drivers would look after him if I sent him back alone. They said they would. I bought his ticket, gave the driver money for his food and pinned a note to him saying who he was, where he was going. And who to contact in an emergency.

I discovered a few days later that he had arrived with all the money I had given the drivers for his food, a big toy truck, and a lot of toy cars.

He told me on the phone that he'd had a lot of fun and that everybody was good to him.

He said that four different drivers had taken care of him. Thank God for those four men wherever they are today.

Meanwhile, the rest of us had gone on to Anderson, California, where Brad had an aunt and uncle we could stay with. When Brad introduced me and the kids to them, a funny look came over their faces. Brad's uncle took him aside, and his aunt began asking me a lot of questions. I don't think we had been expected.

Brad's aunt and uncle owned a restaurant, and they gave him a job in the kitchen. About a week later, his aunt gave him money to rent a house, and I enrolled the kids in school.

Grandma Willis wrote the kids frequently. When I called and let her talk to them, she would ask them, "Don't you want to come back to Grandma's?"

That upset Allen, and, by the time she hung up, he would be crying and asking to go back home to her. He was six, and it was his first year in school.

One day the teacher sent a note home with Allen asking me to come to school the next day. When I got there, Allen had his head on the desk and was crying.

"Why are you crying?" I asked him.

"Mommy, I want to go home to Grandma's house."

I probed a little, asking him why.

"I don't like my shoes anymore. The kids keep asking me when am I going to learn to put my shoes on right. I put my shoes on right, don't I, Mommy?"

He was wearing his corrective shoes, and the kids had been making fun of him.

"Yes, Allen," I said. "Remember we talked about your shoes and why they look that way? I told you other kids would tease you about them. Remember what I told you to tell them?"

"Yes, Mommy. You told me my shoes would fix my feet."

"That's right. Now you stand up and tell the kids that, okay?"

He stood up, wiped his tears away and told the class, "I'm crippled, and my shoes are fixing my feet."

The teacher had tears in her eyes, and she told the kids to stand up and tell Allen they were sorry for making fun of him. They did. The teacher then apologized to me.

Whenever Allen went to a new school, I would talk to his teacher and have her tell the kids about Allen's shoes. We wouldn't usually have any problem. I had done the same thing to this teacher, but she hadn't made the connection between the shoes and his constant crying.

One time after that, Allen wasn't on the school bus when it stopped at the bus stop. I asked the driver if Allen had gotten off somewhere else, but he hadn't noticed. I nearly went crazy. I scoured the neighborhood and finally found him. He had gotten on another bus to go home with a friend.

I was so glad to see him that I couldn't even give him a spanking for what he did. But I did give him a good talking to.

On another occasion it was Lynn who gave me a scare. It was raining hard, and I had gone to the bus stop to pick up the kids, but Lynn didn't get off the bus.

"Where's your sister?" I asked Kay.

"I don't know. I didn't see her get on the bus."

I went flying down the road, looking up and down all the side streets. It was raining so hard I could hardly see, and I was crying nearly as hard inside.

I reached the school and saw her standing in the rain, crying. She was soaked.

"I'm sorry, Mommy," she sobbed. "I missed the bus. I don't like it here. I want to go home to Grandma's."

I hugged her for a long time in the car.

Brad's aunt and uncle didn't have any children of their own, and they thought a lot of mine. His aunt particularly loved Allen. At Christmas she bought all the children gifts and fruit and candy.

Brad's mother began calling. His uncle would come over to the house and tell Brad to call his mother, or so he said. Brad would go to a phone booth to call. When he returned, he would say that the phone call was to his kids and everything was fine.

When I went to the motor vehicle department to get California plates, Brad told me to register in my former name. I thought that was odd and asked him why I couldn't use my married name. Brad said he would tell me later.

We were getting along well as a family. Brad and I had a lot of good times taking the children places. He was always doing things with Allen.

Then one day I got a letter from Gene telling me that the finance company had repossessed the car and that he wanted his money back from Brad. Gene told me he didn't think Brad was who he said he was and that I had better do some checking on him.

I had become very suspicious, and, while Brad was at work, I went through all his personal papers. They were made out in different names.

While he was in bed that night, I looked in his billfold and discovered that the name on the driver's license was different than the name he was now using and the name we had gotten married under.

I woke him up and demanded some answers. He broke down and confessed that he was AWOL from the army and that he already had a wife when he married me. Although they were separated, they had never gotten a divorce. Neither his parents nor his aunt and uncle had known that he had married me. He was using his brother's nickname and his first name.

He had been home on leave when he met me and decided to go AWOL. He said he had fallen in love with me and didn't want to lose me. He said he'd known all along that eventually I'd find out and had been living in fear that the MPs would find him. The calls from his mother had been to warn him about the MPs and to beg him to give himself up.

I told him that under the circumstances, I couldn't live with him anymore and would leave for Indiana as soon as I could get the money together.

I talked to his aunt and told her the whole story. I told the kids that we would pack up and leave on Friday after school. I didn't tell them why. We were all laughing and crying as we packed.

When we got ready to go, Brad had tears in his eyes and told me he was sorry for what he had put us through. I never saw him again.

Chapter Fourteen

We left at midnight because I didn't want to drive the desert during the day. Jackrabbits kept jumping across the road in front of us, and we saw a lot of snakes. The kids were happy to be going home, and by then I was too. We got to laughing and generally having a good time. Lynn, who was about eleven at the time, read the map for me. We drove almost straight through and pulled in about seven on Monday morning.

The kids went running as fast as they could up to the door hollering, "Grandma! Grandma! We're here!" I'll never forget the way her face lit up.

I couldn't stay there because Phil was still living there off and on. So I went to Mother's and went straight to bed. I slept right through the day into the next. Mother said she didn't know if I were dead or alive for awhile. My sisters had come over, but I had never budged.

After I had been home for a week or so, Brad called and talked to my mother. He was back in Rushville and had turned himself in. He was being returned to Germany the next day. He told her how sorry he was for what he had done to me.

I went to visit his wife, told her the story, and asked her to forgive me. She told me she had filed for divorce.

I also went to visit his parents. They couldn't believe their ears, and it was hard for them to accept what Brad had put me through. They told me they were sorry and wished me good luck.

I was twenty-seven.

I had never drank alcohol beverages, taken drugs, or run around. Now that I was single again, I didn't know how to handle myself.

I loved country music and dancing, so one night I went with Gene and his wife to a tavern where there was a country band. I danced and had a ball. I would also go out dancing with two or three girlfriends. It was a way to help me forget the past.

A niece I hadn't seen in years, Sue, moved back into town with her husband, and we began going out on Friday and Saturday nights. Sue told me once that her husband was afraid of graveyards.

On impulse one night as we were returning from a dance, I drove into the race track at the fairgrounds and began racing around and around as fast as I could with the radio blaring. We were jumping up and down, singing and hollering, and having a ball.

I flew off the track and into the graveyard, and Sue's husband began hitting me and screaming at me to get out of there, or he was going to walk home. I stopped the car in the middle of the graveyard and told him to get out. He wasn't about to, so both Sue and I began pushing him out. He grabbed the steering wheel and tried desperately to stay in the car, but we finally got him out.

We shoved him into the mausoleum and shut the door. He was screaming that he could smell the dead. When we let him out, he was as white as a sheet and had peed in his pants. He said Sue and I were crazy and he would never ride with me again.

The newspaper reported the next day that someone had torn up the race track and racing would have to be delayed until it was repaired.

When I went to taverns, it was mostly to dance as I didn't drink very much. It made me too sick. In the beginning I had drank beer and tomato juice together and ended up in the hospital being catheterized, and that was no fun.

My brother Lloyd was divorced by then and was often with me. The owner of one bar told me that I brought in a lot of business for him because I was a dancing fool and everyone wanted to dance with me and sit at my table. I always had a big crowd around me, young and old. We laughed and talked and had a good time. We never had any trouble, just good clean fun.

One night when I went into my favorite tavern, I saw a big long table set up in the middle of the aisle with a sign on it that said: "Reserved for Ruth's party."

"But I'm not having a party," I told the owner.

"You are going to be the life of one tonight," he told me. "Anything you want is on the house."

The table was covered with food people brought in, and all my friends were seated around it. I hadn't known I was that well liked.

I didn't go with married men, not if I knew they were married. I didn't even dance with married men unless they had the permission of their wives. I didn't want to cause any trouble for anybody.

One night I went to a tavern with Louise, her husband, and her son Paul. Phil came in, walked over to our table and said to Paul, "You are sitting with my ex-wife and she has four children by me."

"I know she's your ex-wife," Paul said. "She's also my aunt Ruth."

Phil apologized and had drinks sent to our table. We had them sent back and left. I realized then that I would never be safe from Phil until the day he died.

My favorite tavern was sold, and I started going to Indianapolis. I joined dance contests and always won. I dated a lot of men, and I wasn't any angel. I was out to hurt any man I could.

One Friday night I made dates with seven different men to pick me up at Mother's house. I went out after work and didn't get in until three a.m. Mother was waiting up for me.

"What did you think you were doing making dates with several men at the same time and telling them to pick you up here?" she asked me.

"Mother," I said, "I never thought that they would show up."

"Well, they did. And one stayed a couple of hours talking to me. Don't you ever do that again, Ruthie."

I promised I wouldn't. But I did go out to dinner with men, eat, and then excuse myself and go to the ladies' room. If it had an outside window, I would go out it and leave them sitting waiting for me. One guy I did that to went home and told Mother what I had done. She could hardly believe it.

When I came in, she was still mad at me.

"What is your problem with men?"

"I hate them," I said. "It took only one to hurt me, but I'm going to hurt them all."

"They're not all like Phil," she pointed out. "Someday you may hurt the wrong one."

I thought about what she said, and I did begin treating men a little better.

One night I went to the Lemon Tree Club in Indianapolis with three or four girls. Jerry Lee Lewis was playing there, and we were having a good time dancing and talking. There were four guys at a table across from us, and I danced with three of them.

The fourth one kept coming up and asking me to dance, but he smelled and I kept refusing. I finally told him that he stank and needed a bath. He got mad, broke a beer bottle and started a fight.

A piece of the bottle flew into my upper leg, and, before I knew it, my pretty party dress was covered with blood. The bartender took me to the emergency room where they removed the glass and put four or five stitches in my leg.

We returned to the club. I borrowed a dress from one of the go-go girls and began dancing again. My leg was so numb I couldn't feel anything.

The next day I discovered that I had torn out one of the stitches. My leg hurt so badly that I had to stay home that night. I told Mother that I just didn't feel very good. I have never told anyone in my family what happened to me that night.

About six months after I moved in with Mother, my sister Thelma moved in too. When Mother went to church, Thelma, our brother Albert, and I had many good times together. We would turn the radio on to some country music, and Thelma and I would dance while Albert lay on the couch laughing at us. If an Ernest Tubb song came on, Albert would sing along with the radio.

We had to watch the clock and be sure we had the radio turned off before Mother got home from church. When she got back, we would all sit down with a cup of coffee as Mother told us about the service and began preaching to us. After awhile, we would wander off to bed.

Sometimes if I had a date and decided not to go, I would hide in the bathroom and tell Thelma or Albert to tell the man I wasn't there. Or I would leave before he got there and go next door to Gene's house. It worked for awhile, but Thelma and Albert got tired of lying for me and told one guy that I was over at Gene's.

Then I pulled a trick on all of them. As soon as I saw my date drive up, I would run out the back door and down the alley and walk around the block until I saw him leave.

"Where were you?" Mother asked one time when I pulled that trick. "You weren't at Gene's."

"I guess I forgot to tell you I was going over to the grocery store for some cigarettes. Has he been here already?"

Albert got a big kick out of some of my tricks.

I had a good friend named Karen I ran around with most of the time. She was engaged to Robb, a man in Lexington, Kentucky, who came up to see her on weekends. One weekend he told me he had a friend he wanted me to meet, a police officer he described as "tall and not bad looking."

Karen and I went to Lexington with Robb the next weekend. Saturday night Robb introduced me to a tall man that must have been 6' 7". He looked at me and said, "Robb, where did you find this dish. She looks good enough to eat."

I thought that he looked big enough to do it.

"My name is Ruth," I said.

"Everyone calls me Tubby," he said. He was as skinny as a bean pole. He looked very nice in his black suit. I had on a pink suit, and at least we didn't clash in colors.

We had a good dinner at a nice nightclub, and Tubby was treating me like a lady. The band began playing country music. The first number was a slow one, and Tubby asked me to dance. He held me so close and tight that my face was pressed into his chest, and all I had to hold on to was his hips. I thought that if there were any more dances like that I'd have a broken neck.

The next dance was a fast one. Tubby twirled me around, and I went flying across the room and fell into a couple sitting at a table. Tubby came running over and asked, "Honey, are you hurt?" He apologized to the couple and then told me he was sorry and would be more careful next time.

I was afraid to dance with him again, and we sat out a few dances. Finally he asked to dance another slow one. He had me in a tight clutch, my face pressed to his chest. I looked up and told him he was holding me too tight, and I couldn't breathe. He apologized again.

He was sweet and kind, and I made out the best I could because I didn't want to hurt his feelings. Later, Robb told me that Tubby liked me and asked if I would be willing to go out with him again. I told Robb that I liked tall men but that Tubby was a giant.

"If I danced with him very often, I would have to have my neck in a brace and my legs in a cast. I want to live a little longer."

"Does that mean 'no'?" Robb asked.

"I'm afraid so."

Actually, I preferred going out with a gang of girls and dancing with whomever I pleased. I didn't go out any more on blind dates.

We were a good old bunch who liked to dance to country music. Many of those people are dead now, but I think of them often. Some of them may read this book, and I hope they will remember that I love them all.

I met and dated two men I liked, one a Navy recruiter and the other a factory worker. I dated each of them for a year. I suspected that they were both married, but I never did find out for sure.

Phil and the kids lived with his mother, and I would try to go see them whenever his car wasn't around. One time I didn't see his car, so I went to the door and knocked. Phil's mother opened the door, and I went in. Phil was standing behind his mother, and he slammed his fist into my face and knocked me back out the door. I went home with a bloody nose and black eye.

Another time Phil was there with a girlfriend when I showed up. I thought it was going to be a nice visit, but after awhile he started in on me, pushed me toward the wall and let me have it with a fist upside my head. The kids were scared, and his girlfriend ran outside. I had a knot on my head for a week. I never saw the girlfriend again.

Despite episodes like that, I wouldn't give up on my kids.

One night I felt something cold next to me in bed. I sat up and saw a big black snake with Phil's head. I started screaming for Mother to open the window and let it out. I was still screaming when she shook me awake and told me I was having a nightmare. I had a lot of nightmares about Phil.

I continued visiting the kids whenever I could. One day Grandma and I were having lunch with the kids when Phil came in and sat down with us. After lunch Phil told me he now realized what he had lost and wanted us to get back together. He said he had changed. I told him I didn't trust him and I didn't love him anymore.

Phil jumped up and grabbed me and began hitting me so hard I got dizzy. He said he was going to fix my face so no man would ever look at me. Grandma and Dale were trying to pull him off me. Dale bit him in the leg, and he finally let me go.

My nose was bleeding; I had a cut on my lip; and my eye was swelling. When I got back to Mother's, she called the police. They came to the house and took my statement, but that was the last we heard from them. Albert kept giving me ice for my face. My mother was so mad she could have bitten nails in two. The kids came over to see me a few days later.

I was at work one day when my boss told me my mother-in-law had called and said one of my kids was hurt. I hurried over to Grandma's and discovered that Kay had burned her legs with hot cooking grease. I took her to the emergency room. She had third degree burns.

Grandma and I were fixing lunch one day when Phil came in and started in on me. I had a skillet in my hand, and I hit him with it. Boy, did that shock him. He hit me back, and I picked up a big ash tray and threw it at him. It hit him on his hip bone and really hurt him.

"Well, you're starting to fight me back," he said.

I told him he wasn't really a man because he picked only on weak women who were afraid of him. I added, "I'm not afraid of you anymore, and, if you come at me one more time, I'll run this butcher knife through your guts."

I told him he was never going to stop me from seeing my kids, but that I was tired of him beating on me every time I came over.

"You are scaring the kids," I told him, "and you're going to give your mother a heart attack. We are divorced, and you're going to have to find you another woman to beat on."

Phil went in the living room, settled down in his chair and ordered his mother to fix him something to eat. I told him if he didn't eat at the table, he wouldn't eat at all, but his mother carried the food to him in the living room.

"That's what is wrong with Phil," I told her. "You have spoiled him rotten."

Mother and I were going to the store one day when the back wheel fell off. I had to have the car towed home. The tow truck repairman told me somebody had loosened the lug nuts and beat the rim up. I couldn't prove Phil had done it, but I knew he had.

Another time the car wouldn't start, and I had to have it towed to a garage where the mechanics found that someone had poured sugar into the crankcase and gas tank. The engine was ruined. I sold the car to my cousin for one hundred dollars, and he put a new engine in it.

I couldn't get another car right away and had to walk to work. I was on my way home one day when someone shouted at me to get out of the way. Phil was driving down the sidewalk trying to hit me. I ran into a black tavern.

On another occasion, my sister Louise and I were leaving a restaurant and ran into Phil. He was about to hit me when a friend came out and saw what was happening. He knocked Phil in the head and told him, "Don't you even think about hurting her anymore, or I'll kill you!"

I was becoming afraid of my own shadow. I was afraid to go out in Shelbyville and went out of town when I wanted to dance. The kids were still with Phil's mother, and I was living with my mother, enjoying the single life. Or at least I thought I was.

Chapter Fifteen

One night I met a tall, dark, and cute guy named Stan who just wouldn't leave me alone. He picked me up and took me to work and was back to take me home. I couldn't get rid of him.

One night I took off before he got there because I had a date. We went to a place uptown, and Stan came in and asked me to dance. I told him to go away and leave me alone. The guy I was with told him to get lost.

The next morning Stan came over and told me he was in love with me and wanted to marry me. That floored me. I didn't love him and told him so. After that, however, he went around telling people that we were engaged to be married. We began dating, and I discovered that we did have some things in common.

I told him that I had four kids, and he told me he had a girl who lived with his ex-wife. Stan and I were married in 1966. I thought it would be a chance to get my kids back.

We moved in with his parents as soon as we got married. I didn't like them at all, and, after two weeks, I left him and went back to Mother's.

About a week later, Stan came by to tell me he had found a big house for all of us. I took my kids, and we moved in. I had to change their school. I took them often to see their grandmother when she was alone, and once in awhile I let one of them spend the weekend with her.

It wasn't long before Stan was fired, and I ended up paying all the bills. Eventually he found another job.

I came home from work one day and found Stan on the porch and the police inside talking to the kids. I went in to find out what was going on. Dale's nose was bleeding, and he was crying.

"Mommy, Stan hit me in the nose."

When I asked why, he told me he was hungry when he came home from school and had gone into the refrigerator to get a snack. He said that Stan had told him he couldn't have anything and had hit him. He called the police, he said, because he knew I would.

I didn't have Stan arrested but told him the kids could have a snack anytime and he had better never lay a hand on one of my kids again. He never did, but I was beginning to think I had made a terrible mistake in marrying him.

After that, the kid's didn't like him, and he didn't like them. The kids started going over to Grandma's after school, and I would have to go pick them up. Kay skipped school one day, and, when I got home from work, I found all her clothes gone. She had moved back in with Grandma. Then Dale and Allen said they wanted to move back too, and I gave in and let them. Lynn continued to live with me and Stan. She was never any problem.

In the first year, Stan was fired from three or four jobs. I saw one of his old bosses at the grocery store one night and asked him why he had fired Stan. He told me that it was because Stan wouldn't leave the women alone. I realized then that the marriage was a mistake.

While this was going on with Stan, I was still having trouble with Phil. I took Phil to court for child support one time. At the same time, he signed away his rights to the children. I never did get any money from him. Neither did his mother.

Phil would come over to the house at two or three in the morning drunk and want to see Lynn. I would tell him he could come back at a decent time when he was sober.

One time he showed up drunk in the middle of the night with Dale, Kay, and Allen and wanted Lynn. He wanted to take them all out to the cemetery to stand on Bryan's grave. I begged him to leave Dale, Kay, and Allen with me for the night, but he insisted on getting Lynn.

When he tried to come in after her, I pulled a shotgun on him and told Stan to call the police. Phil took off with my three kids to the graveyard. I sent the police after them, and they reported to me that the kids had been crying and upset because Phil had been telling the kids that I had killed the baby and was no good. They followed him until he left the kids off at Grandma's.

Kay was a beautiful girl and big for her age. She was also stubborn and rebellious. She didn't like housework or cooking. All she wanted to do was play with her girlfriend or go fishing.

When she was fourteen, she ran away and was gone for a week. I looked everywhere for her. When she got back, she told me she had gone to Indianapolis with her boyfriend. I tried to have the boy arrested, but the police said I couldn't since she was willing and no force had been used.

I about lost my mind with worry and had to quit work for awhile. After about a month, Kay began to look very pale and was sick to her stomach.

A short time later she and her boyfriend asked if I would sign for them to get married. I told them no because she was too young. I didn't want my kids to make the same mistake I had.

"Mom, I'm pregnant," Kay said.

I had already assumed that. I told her that she didn't need to ruin her life with a young marriage. I told her we would keep the baby and raise it.

The next day Kay and her boyfriend took me to a judge at the courthouse.

"You know that your daughter is pregnant and she and her boyfriend want to get married?" the judge asked me.

"Yes."

"What do you think about that?"

"I don't like it, and I won't give my approval."

"I'm going to give them the permission to get married," the judge said, and he signed their marriage license. I signed too, and they went ahead and got married. I didn't attend the ceremony, but I did get a beautiful grandson.

Lynn was in high school and had a job at a root beer stand called Bears' Den after school. She got a charge account at a dress shop and bought all her own clothes and school books. She helped me clean house and always did the dishes after supper. I never had to ask her to do anything. She just did it.

Both Stan and I got jobs at General Electric. One day Stan came over to say he had just been fired. On my break, I asked his boss why and was told it was because he wouldn't leave the women alone. That made three or four times he had lost a job over women, and I'd had enough.

We separated, and I sued him for divorce. We had been married only three years.

I didn't have a car, and Lynn and I had to catch a ride to work. Lynn and I had fun living alone. In her last year of high school she had to go to classes only half a day, so she got a job as a PBX operator.

I was working the night shift then, and I began getting phone calls at work telling me one of the kids had been hurt. But when I would rush home to Grandma's I would find that they were all okay. Phil had put some woman up to calling me, and he would then stop by his mother's, knowing I would be there. He was always trying to get me to go with him to a hotel room or meet him in some bar. I asked him when he was going to give up on me, and he told me never, that he would always be behind me and, even when he died, he would come back to haunt me.

It was in late 1969 when Stan and I were separated. I took a leave of absence from General Electric. I was sitting with a girl friend in Lloyds Lounge one Saturday afternoon listening to country music playing on a juke box. A man came up to me and asked me to dance. I danced with him then he asked if he could join us. So we said yes. He said, I'm A. J. Johnson, manager of a restaurant on Vine Street which used to be Taylors Fish fry. He asked me my name, I said Ruth. He looked to be about 20 years older then I. Very well dressed and smelled good. We got to talking and he said the lady he worked for was getting to old to work anymore and he was looking for someone to go into a partnership with him. He told me he didn't have enough money to pay up all the bills she was behind in. She wasn't

paying him at the time but he liked the old lady and wouldn't leave her. She owned the Restaurant and she wanted A. J. to take it over for her. He asked me if I would be interested in a partnership with him since I was on leave from G.E. I asked him how big is the restaurant, he said five big rooms and a bath room. A large parking lot on the side and you can park on the streets in Shelbyville. When you came in the front door there was this big dinning room, a juke box, a small case which held cigarettes, candy, chewing gum and such and on top of it set the cash register. We can seat about 100 people and it had a counter with 12 stools to set at. Behind the counter was a large grill, Bunn coffee makers, and such, which was open all day. Off to the right was another big room which led out to the side door parking lot. The bathroom was also off the dinning room. In the back there were 3 big more rooms, one room filled with two big freezers and a refrigerator. A large kitchen and a dry goods room. The kitchen had a grill, deep fryer and this huge cooking stove with a big oven. I had never seen such a big stove and it had another refrigerator. It had a table where you prepared the food on and there were 3 tubs for washing dishes. One to wash rinse and sanitize them and a huge counter with dish drainers to dry them. The restaurant was well stocked. AJ and I went out to the restaurant and I inspected it from top to bottom. I told him It would have to be cleaned up. I asked him how much money he needed to pay up the back bills. She had a pretty big Phone bill. He told me, so I agreed to a verbal agreement. No contract signed. I was thinking if this didn't work out between us I could leave and not be responsible for any bills. AJ agreed with my verbal agreement on Monday. I had a savings account with General Electric and took out my half of the money we needed. We closed for a week while we cleaned the restaurant. I wanted it spotless and shining. I'm an organizer so I started in the dry goods area, unpacked all boxes and everything had a place and it had better stay in its place or everyone heard about it. I told AJ, I cooked country style food. Ladies, here is a few of my recipes, but if you don't want unexpected company at meal time don't use my recipes. All my vegetables had to be half drained of fluid and cooked with real butter and real potatoes, mashed with half and half cream and real butter, chicken was fried in real lard in an iron skillet, potatoes were fried in bacon grease in an iron skillet. Cornbread was made with half corn meal and half flour with some sugar and bacon grease and it was baked in the iron skillet. I'll have to admit no one knew how to bake biscuits so we ordered can biscuits, I made my own chicken and dumplings with real flour, not biscuits. I cooked a lot of sauerkraut with country style spare ribs, that was served with fried or mashed potatoes and a vegetable, a fruit or pudding cake or pie and a drink for one price. That was a real seller for lunch time or dinner, plus my home made vegetable soup made with real beef pot roast, cabbage, potatoes, tomatoes, onions, and a can of every vegetable we had went into it served with cornbread. AJ's ex-wife made all our pies and cakes, noodles from scratch, very good I might add, all deserts I made. Jell-O with mixed cool whip on fruit was another good seller for us. All my beans, great northern and pinto were cooked either with fresh, not cured, bacon or old joe, some called it, or ham. Green beans and cabbage, we used the same kind of meat or a ham hock. We opened up at 5:AM and I got the bacon and sausage, gravy and biscuits going, plus the fried potatoes, and I fried some sausage, not much, everyone wanted sausage, gravy. We closed at 7:00PM. I talked to AJ and we decided to rename the restaurant, we called it the Horse Shoe Cafe. We placed a Horse Shoe over the front door for good luck. I baked my own baked beans some times out of the beans I cooked. But I hardly had any left at the end of the day. So I used Campbell's pork and beans, I put brown sugar, ketchup, and a little mustard, onions, bacon grease, and fried bacon broken up. Sometimes I used honey they are both good. I also made my own chili, but I'm not going to tell my secrets to it. Very seldom we had anything left over from one day to the next. Our restaurant did a very good business and we were always packed. I made special cornbread with cracklings in it for a few of our customers, little things mean a lot to some people if you just take the time to please them they will keep coming back. All our potato, macaroni salads were all made by hand, back in those days we didn't have any modern equipment like restaurants have today. Nothing came all ready chopped or shredded, we did it all by hand. I made cucumber salad with onions and vinegar, water and a little salt, I made two kinds of slaw, one with vinegar, water and a little sugar, the other with milk, sugar and miracle whip salad dressing. I had a grinder you turned the crank around by hand and I ground up my own cranberries, for awhile I used Mom Willes' recipe made with cranberries, lime or lemon Jell-O, apples and oranges and pecans. Now I buy whole cranberries in a can. I use apples and oranges and pecans. All my salads were put in the refrigerator over night. I made candied sweet potatoes with brown sugar, butter and crushed pineapple. But please drain your pineapple juice off.. I also make candied carrots with brown sugar and butter.. When you have very little left or none at all, that makes me very proud knowing all the hard work I put into my cooking was worth it. I'm a people pleaser and its to late to change now. I did not like one of the waitresses AJ had so one afternoon I went to another small restaurant sat down and a waitress was right there to serve me. Very pretty and polite to me, I watched her work for awhile and then I heard her say to a friend of hers, she had gotten a divorce and with two kids and no support. She was going to need a better paying job but all she knew how to do was waitress work. When she returned to fill up my coffee cup I told her I heard what she told her friend, I said how much are you making here, she told me. I said how would you like to work for me. At the Horse Shoe Cafe on Vine Street and how much pay are you willing to work for. I hired her, her name was Billy Jo, I forgot her last name. I asked when can you start work, she said tomorrow morning if that is OK with you. I told her I would like for her to work with me in the kitchen and we open at 5:00AM and then when we opened for business at 6:00AM she could go on the floor. She didn't have a ride to work so I picked her up. I told her she could work as many hours as she wanted. I paid her good wages. It was as if she was attached to my side, nothing she wouldn't do for me. Billy Jo became my best friend and I loved her very much and I still think about her today and wonder where she is. When we changed the name we added to our sign AJ's Ruth and Billy Jo. Many nights Billy Jo stayed over and helped me prepare food for the next day. I wouldn't get home at night until twelve or one in the morning. AJ cleaned the bath room, sweep and mopped the floors. Everything had to be spotless before we left, we never knew when the health inspector would show up. Then we decided to stay open all night Friday and Saturday night, I went home got a few hours of sleep and opened up again at 12PM, midnight. My daughter Lynn decided she wanted to be a waitress so she worked after school during the week and all night Friday and Saturday night. Lynn made up all my menus for the whole week. Lynn was a very good waitress. Stan was dating a girl named

Dee, she had a day time job but came to me one night when she and Stan came into the restaurant and asks me if I would hire her as a waitress all night Friday and Saturday, she needed extra money because she was divorced with one son. I told her it wouldn't bother me a bit that she was dating my husband. So I hired her, another very good waitress. One Saturday night Stan was bringing Dee to work and when he got out of his car in the parking lot Phil knocked him upside his head. Stan came in with a knot on his head so I told him to go back in the kitchen and I put ice on his head. Then I told him if he wanted to be around Dee he could wash dishes all night which he did a few times. Most of the time he would watch me and Dee. Say one thing to me and another thing to Dee. He said to me he didn't know which one of us he wanted. I told him we were getting a divorce he didn't have a choice.

Sometimes Dale and Allen would walk from their Grandmas' house clear across town to see me. Dale was about 14 or 15 Allen about 10, Dale said Mommy we want to work too. So I told Dale he could clean the bath room, sweep, mope floors, which he did and a good job at that. Allen set on a stool and rinsed dishes, I told him he had to rinse them real good which he did. When they would show up I put them to work and paid them some money. A few times Louise or Kay would come in on Friday or Saturday night and sit at the counter. I would give them something to eat. Kay was about 6 or 7 months pregnant by then, she kept making the coffee for me then stay a few hours and go home. Louise's husband let Louise come and she stayed until 3 or 4 in the morning. One time I fixed her a T-bone steak and she just drank coffee and talked with people she knew. I really enjoyed those days in the restaurant and then AJ started telling people or friends of mine I would sit and talk with I was his girl and we were going to be married. He became very jealous and possessive over me. I told him I was still married and wasn't interested in him or any one. Besides AJ was about 20 years older then I was. Stan and Dee broke up their relationship and Stan started coming in with a new girl friend thinking that would get me and Dee jealous but we would pay no attention to them and they would leave. Phil started coming in after the taverns closed and would set on a stool at the counter drinking coffee and watching me and Lynn, Lynn was scared to death of him and I was too. I hired my brother Lloyd as a cook, he was a real good cook and he and his wife moved in with Lynn and I. When I seen Phil come in I would tell Lloyd. All he had to do was make sure Phil seen him. After a few hours Phil would leave, he was scared of Lloyd and never started any trouble in the restaurant. I sensed trouble coming down the road with AJ, Stan and Phil so I told AJ I wanted out of the partnership and he could have it. I left the business and returned to work at General Electric on the 4 to 12 shift as a machine operator. Stan and I moved to Virginia, Lynn stayed on as a waitress, she told me AJ turned the extra room off the dinning room into a dance floor and hired a country band to play on Friday and Saturday nights. Back in those days no drinking was allowed in any restaurant in Shelbyville. Now that has all changed and I'm sorry to hear that now parents can take their children out to eat and see their parents drinking at the same time. No wonder we have so many teenagers drinking today. I'm proud to say my children never seen that out of me. All my children love my cooking because I learned it from Mom Willis and I make sure when each one of them is coming I'll fix their favorite foods and I still make Mom Willis' home made cheese cake which we all loved. The restaurant AJ and I had is now a church, praise God. It didn't turn into another tavern. I got many compliments on my fried chicken and cooking many times customers gave me a tip, now that's an honor.

Stan came by one day and said he was moving to Florida and asked me to go with him. I thought it would be a chance to leave Shelbyville and get out of Phil's sight, so I agreed. I dropped my divorce suit.

Lynn moved in with Norma to finish high school, and Stan and I went to Florida. But when Stan got fired from another job over a woman, I left him and went to Virginia to live with Glenda. Stan followed me to Virginia. I tried one more time, but Stan kept up his old tricks, and I finally divorced him in 1973.

While waiting on the divorce to be final, I got a phone call telling me that my brother Albert had died. Glenda and I went home to the funeral. That was a very sad day for all of us. Albert was only fifty-two. I still miss him.

Chapter Sixteen

I thank God every day for the fact that I am here and for the relationship I have with my four kids today.

I didn't know everything my kids had gone through until long after I divorced Phil, and I am still finding out disturbing new things.

Kay has told me that Phil started to molest her when she was about nine years old. He would get her out of bed at night and take her out into the country or to a motel to molest her. And when she was nineteen, Phil raped her.

I've never understood how Phil's mother could let him take a little girl out of her bed in the middle of the night and not tell me or call the police on him.

Allen has told me how Phil used to bend his arms behind his back and force his head to the ground. Allen has told me about the time that he and his father had been out talking and drinking. When he got up to go home, his father jumped him from behind. He said he thought then that it was pretty bad when you couldn't trust your back to your own father. Allen doesn't trust anyone to this day. He holds everything in and won't talk about his feelings.

Kay has told me how Phil would beat them upside their heads with his fist. She said that Phil beat on Dale the worst and would try to get him to fight him like a man.

Kay told me about the time that she and her son were whispering with Grandma on the couch one day while Phil was watching TV. Phil told them to shut up, but her son kept whispering. Phil picked him up and slammed him on the floor so hard that Kay was afraid he might have broken the boy's back. She picked him up and ran out of the house.

One day Lynn called me in Virginia and wanted to come. I was very happy when I went to the bus station to pick her up. She had a black eye, and her glasses were broken. When I asked her who had done that to her, she said it was her dad. When he hit her, he told her she was just like her mother. I wanted to go back to Indiana and have him arrested, but Lynn told me no because she didn't want any more trouble with him.

Lynn went back to Indiana and joined the Air Force. After she got out, she went to college and graduated top of her class. I'm very proud of her.

Phil raped a young girl and went to prison for two years. He should have gone to prison for what he did to his own daughters, but at least there was one time he didn't get by with his crimes. Shortly after he got out in 1986, the Lord struck him down with a heart attack because He knew he would never change. He was only fifty-two.

Looking back on my life with Phil, I am overwhelmed with anger. Writing this book is the only way I can let some of that anger out.

Phil got away with too much with the kids, with his mother, and with me. When the kids were little, Phil never mistreated them around me, and I would never have dreamed he could do such awful things.

I've always tried to be a loving, kind, and understanding mother, and I always believed my children and thought they could tell me anything. But they knew the truth about Phil would hurt me, so they didn't tell me a lot of things until after he died.

They were also afraid of him. He would tell them and his mother that if they ever told on him, he would kill them and me. The kids were scared to death of him, afraid he would make good on that promise.

I wish I could take away all the pain that my children have felt and still feel. When Kay told me how her dad had molested her, it felt as if somebody had thrust a knife into my heart.

We all sleep a lot better now. We don't have to watch our backs or worry about what he will do next.

I used to tell Phil that he was a devil's angel. He thought that was funny. I know now that is exactly what he was.

I wish there had been homes for battered women and their children then. I would have been the first one there with four kids.

We did have some good times. Kay remembers an Easter, for example, when Grandma, Grandpa and I took them to the fairgrounds for an Easter egg hunt. Grandpa had the biggest time running around helping the kids fill their baskets.

The good times didn't often include Phil, although Kay remembers a time when we lived in a house behind the hospital that Phil bought them all the biggest Easter baskets he could find.

There were a lot more bad times than good, however. Kay has told me that when they were living with Grandma, Phil came in one Christmas and tore up the tree and house, screaming all the while. He would come in late at night and get Grandma and all the kids up, line them up on the couch and would preach the Bible at them or rant about whatever he was mad about. It would go on for hours.

Phil's family was among the finest, and I had great respect for them. They even got in harm's way trying to protect me. They did not deserve a son like Phil. When he spent six months in prison for abusing his mother, she had a psychiatrist examine him. The psychiatrist told her that Phil had a split personality and if he were drinking or taking drugs, he could be dangerous.

When I go home to Indiana for a visit, the memories are still there, and sometimes I think I can feel his presence. It gives me cold chills.

Chapter Seventeen

I met my current husband in Woodbridge, Virginia, in October 1973. My cousin Jack Spurlin was a country singer who could sing like Elvis Presley. I went to the Hillbilly Heaven Club to hear him sing one night. I had bleached my hair blonde and was dressed in a two-piece blue suit and baby doll high heel shoes to match. A lot of men told me how nice I looked. I was alone, so I sat with the waitress.

A man came up to me and asked me to dance. I danced with him but didn't really pay him much attention. I didn't even know what he looked like.

Later in the evening a man came up and kissed me on the cheek and said he was leaving. I didn't know who he was.

I got hungry and left the club and went to Lum's Restaurant It was packed. A man came up and invited me to sit with him and his friend.

"My name is Tim," he said, "and this is Ron. What's your name?"

"Ruth," I answered.

"What's a good looking girl like you doing out alone?"

I told him I had just got divorced and was thinking about going back to Indiana. Ron dismissed himself to make a phone call, and, while he was gone, Tim told me that they both worked for the FAA as air traffic controllers, he told me Ron was divorced.

"He's a very nice guy," Tim said, "and he needs someone nice."

I didn't think very much about that, but, when Ron came back to the table and told Tim he had to work the next day, I suddenly realized that Ron was the man who had kissed me on the cheek at the club.

Ron paid for my breakfast and bought me a pack of gum. Then he asked for my phone number, and I gave it to him.

We started dating and had some good times together. He loved country music and loved to dance. I felt very proud when I was with him. He was sweet and kind and the most gentle person I had ever met. He treated me like a lady, and I realized he was the man I had always wanted.

We were married in January 1974. He is my husband, my lover, and my best friend. He has given me everything I ever wanted. He treats my four children as if they were his own, and they all love him.

He has been the only man in my life for the eighteen years we have been married. He made up for all the hurt and pain I have gone through.

The first Christmas we were married, Ron asked me what I wanted for Christmas. I told him that I wanted a Raggedy Ann doll. He gave me the biggest one he could find. I had waited thirty-six years for a doll of my own. My Raggedy Ann is over eighteen years old now.

I have a second doll now. It was given to me seven years ago by a sweet and lovely elderly lady in a nursing home I was working in. The lady has passed away, but every time I look at that doll I think of her. I will cherish both dolls as long as I live.

I get back to Indiana now and then. Two years ago we drove through Marietta, Indiana. I saw two of my cousins, Martha and Doris, standing in a side yard talking, and saw another cousin, Evelyn, standing on her front porch. We were just passing through and didn't stop to talk to anyone. Marietta hasn't changed much. They have a fire department now and a few more houses. The house I grew up in has been torn down.

Shelbyville is twice as big as it was when I left it in 1970. I go home often to see my family and children who live there. When we go shopping or out to eat, I have never seen anyone I knew when I lived there. But the old part of the town is the same, and it is still home to me. There is a square in the middle of town in which people sell their vegetables in the summer. My daddy used to sell his vegetables in front of the courthouse.

One time when I was home and getting ready to go back to Florida, we stopped and got a big bag of good old Indiana tomatoes to take back with us. They were really good. You can't beat the garden vegetables from Indiana.

Ron and I had made a trip back to Indiana before Phil died. We were sitting in Mother's living room talking when someone tossed a brick through the glass in the kitchen's back door. Luckily nobody was in the kitchen at the time, or someone could have been seriously hurt. We never found out for sure who did it, but Phil always knew when I was in town. After that we parked our car behind Norma's house so Phil couldn't see it. Even though Phil is dead now and I am, on the whole, very happy and satisfied with myself, sometimes I still think Phil has found a way to come back. When Ron and I lived in Virginia, he spotted a big black snake on the patio. He went out to kill it, but it turned on him and started chasing him. It got away. In Florida, I saw two black snakes in the yard. Ron killed one of them with a shovel, but the other got away. And, back home in Indiana, I was putting flowers on Bryan's grave when I saw a black snake crawling around one of the stones. I got out of there in a hurry. Every time I see a black snake, I think about that dream I had about Phil, and it gives me the shakes. I wonder if Phil hasn't come back as a black snake.

Epilogue

At this writing, there are only five of us girls left. Thelma and all my brothers are dead now. Mother died in April of 1991. She was ninety-four. When I go home now, nothing is the same.

Mother suffered and carried a heavy cross before she died and was saved by the grace of God. Erva said that Mother had at least three or four miscarriages and that Erva and Thelma saved her life after an attempted abortion. They elevated her feet and rubbed her. Erva said Dr. Cohee told Mother to thank her girls that she was still alive. Daddy had been drunk and told them to let her die. The doctor said it was a miracle she didn't.

When she got married herself, Erva said, Daddy and Mother would bring us kids to her house in Shelbyville and leave us for days while he was on a drunk, and even we younger children understood Mother's suffering. Erva said that Daddy asked Mother to forgive him before he died, and she did.

I haven't seen my sister Erva since 1979. I miss being close, but I do talk to her on the phone. She has found out recently that she has a large aneurysm in her heart that can't be operated on. It is a time bomb waiting to go off, and we may lose our oldest sister. She is seventy-six. We are all praying for her.

Norma and Louise took us in too when things got really bad, even though they both had families of their own to take care of. They did what they could to help us, and I love them very much.

While I was writing this book, I learned some new things about my family as my children and sisters shared their stories with me.

Norma and I were both strict with our children. We never abused them, but we did spank their little behinds. I never spanked them hard enough to leave marks, just hard enough to let them know they had to mind me. Sometimes I used a switch, but only on their behinds.

We all keep our houses just as clean today as we did when we were growing up. My neighbors couldn't understand how I could keep a clean house with four kids, and, in truth, it wasn't easy. I would get only five or six hours of sleep a night, but I always took care of my kids. They were my whole life.

I was always up at 5:30 a.m. and had a wash on the line before the kids got up to go to school at 7:30. When they went back to school after lunch, I would lie down for an hour before going to work at three.

Norma had five kids and worked in a factory. She had a babysitter and worked very hard in her home after work. She took very good care of her kids. Junior helped a great deal. There wasn't anything he wouldn't do to help her.

Norma has glaucoma now, just like Mother did. Mother had been blind for years before she died. Norma has had one cornea transplant and has been advised she needs the other eye done. We are all worried about her. Junior is very sick and bedridden and keeps Norma busy taking care of him. It seems as if our family is fading away fast.

Glenda's husband died, and, in 1981, she and her youngest son came to live with us in Florida. She became very sick shortly after she arrived, and I took her to a doctor who told her she had an intestinal infection. He gave her some medication, but she kept getting worse and I wanted to take her to the hospital.

She stubbornly refused, but I told her she was going if Ron had to pick her up and carry her out. The emergency room was packed, and I went up to the desk and asked for a wheelchair. The woman took one look at Glenda and wheeled her into a room. A doctor said she had an intestinal blockage and needed immediate surgery. She came through the surgery fine, but the surgeon said if she hadn't had it, she wouldn't have lived another two days.

Glenda lives nearby now, and we see each other often. Sometimes we laugh about how stubborn she is.

Three of my children are married and doing well. Dale is divorced.

I have five beautiful grandchildren and am excited that one of them, Amy, is giving me a great grandchild. Roger goes to Ball State College in Indiana. Jo Lynn takes dancing lessons. Rick enjoys farming. Dan is now twelve. Since he was born deaf, keeping in touch with him takes a bit of doing, but we work things out. When he wants to talk to Grandma, he has his mother call me, and she tells me what he says and tells him what I say.

I don't interfere in my children's marriages or tell them how to raise their children.

My best friend, Beth, died in a car accident in 1974, and Rex died from a heart attack in 1985. The last time I was home, I saw Phil's old friend Ben. He and his wife have one daughter. He told me he thinks about me often, and I still think of him.

My life was a nightmare for thirty-six years, and sometimes I still dream I see Phil's fist coming at me. Or I dream that I'm knocking on doors and nobody will help me or let me in. But I have learned a few things.

What Mother always said is true: life is what you make it, and, if you don't like it, change it. I discovered that sometimes means we have to change ourselves because we can't change others. I have changed. When I have problems today, I face them and act on them. I settle them once and for all.

And when I have bad dreams, I just say a prayer. God always answers, and I go peacefully back to sleep.

Life is beautiful, and you get out of it what you put into it and how you play it. Love, sex, and marriage are beautiful if you both want the same thing and treat each other as you want to be treated. Marriage is 99.99 percent togetherness. It won't work any other way.

Even a poor girl like me can accomplish something if she wants to badly enough. If you give from the heart, you will get back ten fold.

I worked all my life for others, but eventually I went to school to be a nursing assistant, and, when I got my diploma in 1985 from Indian River Community College, Fort Pierce, Florida I graduated number three from the top of my class and began working for myself. I took care of the elderly in nursing homes, and I worked private duties in homes and hospitals. I have worked for some of the finest nursing homes in Florida and for some of the finest nurses.

My teacher provided me with very good training, and I wouldn't have missed it for the world. I enjoyed that more than anything I have ever done. It gave me great pleasure to serve others.

For a couple of years I worked part-time as a certified nurse's aide and part-time in a beauty salon as a shampoo girl. I found a family away from home in Mechele de Salon and made new friends I still treasure.

During my nursing career I assisted in the care of my mother-in-law and father-in-law. My father-in-law died in 1986, and I quit working in 1990 to continue with the care of my mother-in-law, who lived to be ninety-five.

In 1996 Ron and I moved to Tennessee where I applied for my CNA license to continue the work I love. In August 1998 I went to work as a certified nursing assistant for Fort Sanders Sevier Medical Center in Sevierville, Tennessee. I have fulfilled one of my dreams: to work in a hospital. I work with some of the best nurses, who have trained me well and become my friends. The best part is working one-on-one with my patients and seeing them get better each day and then taking them out in wheelchairs to their cars when they are discharged. I'm there to give them a hug and a kiss, to wish them well, and to say "God bless you."

Ron and I love living in the Smoky Mountains of Tennessee enjoying all the festivals and handicraft shows and taking in the beautiful scenery and, of course, going to Dollywood.

Writing this book has been so hard that I have sometimes gotten sick to my stomach to the point I threw up. I have cried and paced the floor. I have had nightmares about the past and had trouble sleeping at night.

I would get depressed and have to stop writing for a couple of weeks at a time.

I learned some hard lessons that I hope I can pass on. If this book helps just one fourteen-year-old girl or a battered woman or an abused child, then I have accomplished my purpose.

My advice to a young girl who thinks she is in love is to please stay in school. Don't make the mistakes I did.

And I want to urge any woman who is hit by a man to get out of the relationship immediately. The first time he hits you, leave him. He will never change.

If you are an abused child, find an adult you can trust--a teacher, a social worker, a minister--and tell him or her the whole story.

I realize now that I was far too young to get married. But I was desperate to get away from the house, and Daddy was glad to see me go. He told Mother that if I was old enough to bleed I was old enough to marry.

Phil totally controlled me and the kids. It was as if I were under his spell or was a robot whom he could control by pushing buttons. He told me once that the children and I were his possessions, that he could do anything he wanted to us and no one could stop him.

I was young and naive and had no place to go with young kids When I went to my sisters, he would follow me and often cause trouble there.

I did everything possible to keep him from getting upset. I never started an argument with him, and I tried to keep the kids quiet whenever he was home.

To escape him I finally had to leave Shelbyville, leaving my children behind. It's true that they were all teenagers by then and were living with their grandmother, but I still felt as if I were deserting them, even though I think they would have stayed with Grandma anyhow. At least they were all together and not in separate foster homes.

They always knew where I was, and I wrote a lot of letters and called them often on the phone. I never missed one of their birthdays or Christmas.

I know that Phil sometimes took his anger out on the kids because I wasn't there because in his sick mind it was a way of hurting me. He fed my kids with all kinds of lies about me, trying, for example, to make them believe it was my fault when I left them.

I feel as if I have been locked up in prison for thirty years for what I had to do to save my own life. I won't ever get over the feelings of guilt that I deserted my kids, but I wrote this book to tell the truth and explain why I had to do what I did. I pray my children will understand.

It's as if I have been living a double life, an external life without Phil and an internal one where he is still very much with me. But it's time now to let Phil go, if I can.

After writing this book I thought I could get Phil out of me. I wish I could just take an eraser and erase him from my memory and get the feeling of his hands off my face and body. I wish I could reach down my throat to my heart and rip him out to stop the pain and suffering. I am on three different medications, and all they do is keep me glued together. Without them and the help from God I would fall to pieces and end up in a mental hospital. Phil was a jack of all trades, master of one--haunting me just as he said he would.

Now that I have let all my feelings out, I have hope, and God has given me peace and comfort. And I have love.

My children never knew what a real father was until I married Ron. Now they have the best they could ever ask for.

Society is finally waking up to the problem of child abuse and battered wives, but we have a long way to go.

If people don't get help, they can do desperate things. More and more women have been killing the men who have battered them for years. Even children are now killing the parents that abused them to the point they felt they had no choice.

I understand where the battered ladies in prison who finally had enough and struck back are coming from. I've been there too. I could have been their cell mate if it had kept up. But I was lucky; God took him first. Women are weaker than men and can't defend themselves physically. Too often the law is no help, and, when the women defend themselves the only way they can, the police come and put cuffs on them. But never give up hope, and keep praying for justice. I pray you all will be free soon. God bless you.

Sure, we have more men in jail for child and spouse abuse. But most of them will be out in six months or a year, and they haven't learned a thing.

We do have shelters now for battered women and children. Thank God someone saw the need for them.

The misuse of alcohol and drugs by my father and husband were at the bottom of most of the tragedies of my life. My father's alcoholism is what nearly got my mother killed and was the reason that each one of us girls left home and got married very young.

My husband's alcohol abuse forced me to flee to save my own life, leaving behind the most precious things in my life, my children.

I get by day by day with God's help. He is my hope and my answer to everything.

As the final pages are being written I found myself attending the funeral of one of my older sisters, Louise. A sister who has always been a bonding and healing source within our family. As she was put to rest she was surrounded by the remainder of her beloved family members and of her circle of friends. Her love for nature, flowers, birds and many other forms of creation reminded all of us who she was in life and how much she will be missed. Goodbye Louise.

In Memory of Bryan
Empty Arms

I went to Heaven to look for my son Bryan. I found myself walking down this bright and shining, beautiful path, with beautiful flowers of all sizes. I thought to myself what a beautiful home this place is, but I wasn't interested in the flowers. It seemed like I walked a long distance before I saw many men walking toward me on my left side. Each one nodded their head and started on by me. I said "stop! I'm looking for my son Bryan, do you know him?" It seemed like a very long path and then I met Peter, John, Matthew and Luke. I met so many men who I knew from the Bible. Each and every one told me to keep walking. I thought this path had no end to it, I was getting tired, but was anxious to find Bryan. I had to find my son.

I wouldn't stop walking. All of a sudden appeared Jesus at the end of the line of men I had passed Jesus said, "Woman what are you doing here? You haven't been called yet." I said, "I'm looking for my son." Jesus said, "keep looking." I found myself all alone walking down this beautiful path with all these beautiful flowers, and so many beautiful flower gardens. It seemed so long and it took me hours before I came up on this young man standing in a beautiful tiny little flower garden. I thought to myself he looks like my son Allen. I heard this voice. "Mother, I am Bryan." I said I was looking for my baby son who was still born at birth. I said you are a grown man. He said, "Mother, I am your baby son who died before my time." I said, "Bryan you must have died a terrible death." He said, "Mother we both felt a lot of pain." I said, "I'm sorry I wanted you and loved you when you were inside me, we were one at that time."

He said "Mother I love you. I've seen my brothers and sisters who loved me and never knew me. I've seen my father who never wanted me. Mother I've seen you many times with tears flowing down your face. I feel your pain. I feel your broken heart. I see you and the beautiful flowers you put upon my grave. I know you love me because I was never forgotten." We both wrapped our arms around each other so tight. It was like we never wanted to let go. All of a sudden Bryan disappeared out of my arms.

Then it came to me all the beautiful flowers I passed along the way, the little one's were still born babies who died before their time. Jesus said, "Woman you needed not walked so far. If only you had paid more attention to my tiny little beautiful flowers." Then I woke up and realized it was only a dream. I sat up in my bed and cried.

To all the Mothers who have lost a baby before its time, remember they are all up in heaven as tiny little flowers just like mine. What a beautiful and wonderful dream I know in my heart it will come true.

I'll never forget the day my brother-in-law Bob came to take me home from the hospital. It seemed like such a long drive. I sat in the back seat looking out the car window. I was going home without my precious son. I had all these mixed feelings stirring up inside me, I was hurting, sad, lonely, empty inside. Until my time comes as life goes on for me, I still have empty arms.

Sadly missed, with all our love your Mother, brothers, and sisters.

Afterward

Who am I?

My name is Ruth M. Spurlin. Am I who I say I am? Yes and no. If I were an alcoholic or a drug abuser, no. I would be Ruth M. Spurlin and so-and-so--another person inside me would come out. I tried alcohol, but, thank God, it gave me alcohol poisoning, and I ended up in the hospital. I was so sick I wished I were dead. I never did use drugs.

When I was being abused, I was Ruth M. Spurlin. I was very shy and timid, always obeyed my husband, never talked back--a good wife and mother. I shared my feelings only with God and my family. Who else would believe me or understand? Many times I wanted to tell my doctor, but I was too ashamed. My family couldn't help me, but God knew it all and spared me my life and brought me through until the end. God knew when the end would come, but I didn't.

Many times I looked into a mirror with my face all black and blue and swelled up, and I asked myself, who am I? Through thirteen years and many beatings, a nervous breakdown, and the death of my son I took my pain and my bruises and locked them up inside me--never to tell anyone. I built a wall around my heart. I said, "Heart, he didn't really mean to hurt me, or he didn't really mean what he said." I would talk to my heart and say it will be all right; please don't hurt. When I went to bed, I would pray to God, please don't let him come home tonight if he is drunk and hurt me. I would stay awake all hours of the night and pray until God gave me peace and let me fall asleep. I was so frightened, like a little child afraid of the dark. I became cold inside and had no feelings. My heart was empty. I decided to lock up my life and start a new one. I talked to my heart but forgot to talk to God. I became a different person, and again I asked my heart who am I?

Soon I didn't like this other person and went to see a doctor. I told him I was an abused wife one time, and he said to me, "We all have been abused in one way or another." He had no time to listen to me, but I knew what was wrong with me. I was very nervous and depressed and hurting inside. I needed someone to talk to and the right medications to help me through this. Later I found the right doctor whom I could talk to and who listened to me. He put me on the right medication and unlocked my heart, and I threw away the key. I told him things I never told anyone until I wrote my book. Who am I? I'm not shy or timid, and I don't always obey. I talk back. I hold nothing in. I say what I think straight to the point.

There is no medication or cure for the kind of pain or heartache that I and my children have gone through. But I was a battered wife, and my children were abused. All from the effects of alcohol and drugs.

Who is so-and-so? It could be you. If you are an alcoholic or a drug user, you really don't know how much hurt and pain you inflict on others. Do you really want to be a so-and-so, or do you want to become a different person? Do you want to abuse your spouse and children? Alcohol and drugs are real killers of love for yourself and for innocent people. Please get help.

Am I who I say I am? YES, I AM.

I'm a loving wife and mother who has been to the school of hard knocks--much more educated and wiser now and someone who wants to help make a difference in someone's life, because I care about you.

A Letter to My Four Kids
April 1992

I have all this guilt built up inside me.

I feel you loved your grandmother more than you loved me. What happened to you was my fault. I wasn't there to protect you when you needed me. You were all with me in my heart every minute of the day and night. I could hardly sleep at night worrying about you kids.

I have terrible nightmares in which somebody is hurting one of you kids and I can't get to you. I have dreamed that one of you was killed in an accident and another was missing and I couldn't find you. I was always searching for you.

One night I dreamed I was your big sister and drove over and had dinner with you. Then I went home. One time I dreamed I was a kangaroo, and, when something scared me, I gathered you all up in my pouch and hopped away.

Then one night I dreamed that I had finally found all of you kids, and I was happy at last.

I hope you will forgive me. I wasn't gone forever; I was just lost for awhile while running for my life from your father.

I was a very young mother. I started a family at sixteen, and I was just a baby having babies.

I loved your grandmother very much and always will. I feel she treated me more like her daughter than a daughter-in-law, and she was just raising her second family. I feel she stole your love from me and didn't let me raise my own kids.

After she died, I felt as if I had finally got my kids back after all those years. I feel your grandmother did for me and you what she thought was best for all of us because your father wasn't doing it for us.

I was then and still am the only mother you will ever have.

With all my love,
Mother

A Letter to My Husband, Ron

My life with you has been very exciting. Never any planning--just pack the suitcase, and let's go. I never knew where we were going until we got there. Our life has not been all wine and roses. I was not the easiest person to get along with.

When I decided to write my book, you took on the job of typing it for me, and many times I saw tears flowing down your cheeks. And many times you said, "That's it. I can't go on." After a few days went by, however, you would say, "Give me what else you have written." And after awhile it happened all over again, "That's it. No more." When we finally got finished, you had lived my life with me all over again. You know me inside and out. You stood by me and showed me what true love and marriage is all about: treating each other as we want to be treated and together until the end.

Thank you. You are still the one I am in love with.

Your wife,

Ruth

Ron became ill in 1994 and he thought it would be best to move me back home to Shelbyville to be near my sisters and children. We moved to Shelbyville and bought a home and moved into it in February 1995. I had many panic attacks, in the grocery stores and clothing stores and would leave the shopping carts sitting and run out of the stores. I remember when in a grocery store I got in line to pay for the groceries when a man came up behind me, he stood so close to me that I could feel his breath on my neck, I felt fear and had a panic attack, I told the girl "I'm sorry" and left the cart with the groceries sitting and ran out of the store. When I got home I told Ron what had happened and from that time on he took me shopping.

Phil's grave was up on a hill over looking our baby's grave. One day I went to put flowers on my baby's grave I felt fear and thought Phil was going to come up out of his grave and get me and I had a panic attack. I had panic attacks everywhere I went. I had nightmares about Phil. He haunted me every where I went. I told Ron I didn't think I could live there any longer.

Ron had to take me to just about everywhere I wanted to go. I felt safe when he was with me. I had to be put on medication for these panic attacks and we knew then that we made a mistake by moving there and decided to put the house up for sale.

In 1996 we sold the house and moved to Tennessee in the foothills of the Smokey mountains. In 2001 I had a lot of knots coming on my left ear that was very painful and my head started shaking. I went to see my doctor and he didn't know what the knots were and run tests on me to see why my head was shaking. He couldn't find any reason for my head to shake. He sent me to a dermatologist surgeon and she said I would have to have surgery on my ear. I asked her what caused the knots on my ear and caused my head to shake. She said it is called Boxer's ear and asked me if I ever had trauma to my face or head, I told her then that I had many beatings and was abused by my first husband. I have had surgery twice on my left ear. She told me the trauma to my head was called tremor's causing my head to shake and advised me to stay on the medication my doctor had me on. I told her I was abused back in the 1950s and 1960s, she said I would be surprised to what might show up later in life as I get older, that really shocked me to hear that.

My name is Ruth M. Spurlin Klein

There are two kinds of abuse, Physical and Verbal!

I'm very excited to be here tonight. I call this night my feelings inside coming out night. I have never been to a wife abuse meeting before. Up until now and after I wrote my book in 1994. I was not sure I could talk about it at least in public or a group of people. But every time I picked up a news paper and read about a woman or child being abused, even women being killed by their husbands or ex-husbands. Then I turn on the TV and here all these abuse stories then one night on the 60 minute program they showed all these women in prison for killing there husband to stop the abuse. One woman was 70 years old serving life. She had already been in prison for years. My heart really went out to these women. I have collected several news paper stories from Florida. Then while living in Florida the news had a judge on TV the judge said they were setting up special classes for judges to learn how to deal with domestic abuse. why has it taken so long for the law to take such classes Didn't they learn anything in law school about abuse. It has been going on since the 1930's and 40's as I know of my Mother was abused back then. But the law didn't want to get involved. Many times I called the police, but all they would do is talk to my husband tell him to keep his hands off me and settle down. I filed many charges against him. They always told me we can't find him. Well that is because they don't look very hard. I even found him for the police. But they did nothing. I quit watching the news and quit watching the talk shows and quit reading the news paper because it upset me to much to listen to it any more. and nothing being done. I was away for three days at my stepsons' house for thanksgiving when I returned home there was this free news paper in my mail box. "Domestic abuse problem or past time." I picked up the phone and talked to the dean Paul Goldberg continuing educator of Roane state college and he gave me the phone number for me to get in touch with Sandra Boyce at YWCA in Oak Ridge. I'm 60 years old and I'm tired of living and hiding in a shell. So now I'm ready to get involved in a wife abuse center and to help in any way I can. This is almost the end of the 90's and abuse is worse now then its ever been. I don't know how to solve it. But I know for sure we have to keep talking about abuse. We have to be heard in the high schools and Colleges. Maybe even in the 7th and 8th grades. Maybe my book when it comes out will help in education. We who have been abused can't let this be a pastime. It is a very serious problem. It is affecting our children. It has mine and what a better time to start a education program in our schools.

This is the present and we who have been abused must stick together and start fighting to stop abuse. Wife abuse is a life time sentence without serving life in a prison. From being abused for 13 years I have what the doctors call post stress syndrome. I'll always be on medication the rest of my life. Please don't take matters into your own hands and end up in a prison, get out now. Now we have shelters to go to and the law which seems to understand our problems more now. Thank you for listening to me. If you decide to get out don't go back, it will get worse. Abusers never change, at least mine didn't. Maybe if we can educate young men and our children we might have a chance for others in the future. Just maybe we can put abuse in the past. You may not want to hear this but lets don't forget men, they are being abused by women also physically and verbally. Just because they are grown men they don't have to take it and sit back and do nothing. Let them join us, they have feelings and pain and their hearts ache like ours.

Thank you for listening, God Loves you and I do to.

About The Author

Ruth Spurlin, born to an alcoholic father and a strict disciplinarian mother. Living in poverty, she went to work at the age of nine as a farm hand. Married at fourteen convinced she would be moving from poverty and fear, to a new hope of joy with a loving husband. However, she found herself living in more fear and desperately trying to protect herself and her children from a husband who frequently beat her, once so badly he killed their unborn baby. This true story of her struggles to save her life and protect her children carries a message for young girls and women to read before they make the mistakes she made.

www.ingramcontent.com/pod-product-compliance
Lightning Source LLC
Chambersburg PA
CBHW051431280526
45785CB00003B/1245